I DO!

THE LOVE STORY

Until Death Do Us Part

GAIL R. WRIGHT

TRILOGY
A WHOLLY OWNED SUBSIDIARY OF TBN

PROFESSIONAL PUBLISHING MEETS POWERFUL PROMOTION

Trilogy Christian Publishers
A Wholly Owned Subsidiary of Trinity Broadcasting Network
2442 Michelle Drive
Tustin, CA 92780
Copyright © 2025 by Gail R. Wright
All Scripture quotations, unless otherwise noted, taken from THE HOLY BIBLE, NEW INTERNATIONAL VERSION®, NIV® Copyright © 1973, 1978, 1984, 2011 by Biblica, Inc.® Used by permission. All rights reserved worldwide.
Scripture quotations marked AMP are taken from the Amplified® Bible (AMP), Copyright © 2015 by The Lockman Foundation. Used with permission. www.Lockman.org.
Scripture quotations marked MSG are taken from *THE MESSAGE,* Copyright © 1993, 2002, 2018 by Eugene H. Peterson. Used by permission of NavPress. All rights reserved. Represented by Tyndale House Publishers, Inc.
Scripture quotations marked NASB are taken from the New American Standard Bible® (NASB), Copyright © 1960, 1962, 1963, 1968, 1971, 1972, 1973, 1975, 1977, 1995 by The Lockman Foundation. Used with permission. www.Lockman.org.
Scripture quotations marked KJV taken from The Holy Bible, King James Version. Cambridge Edition: 1769.
Scripture quotations marked NKJV are taken from the New King James Version®. Copyright © 1982 by Thomas Nelson. Used with permission. All rights reserved.
All rights reserved, including the right to reproduce this book or portions thereof in any form whatsoever.
For information, address Trilogy Christian Publishing
Rights Department, 2442 Michelle Drive, Tustin, CA 92780.
Trilogy Christian Publishing/ TBN and colophon are trademarks of Trinity Broadcasting Network.
For information about special discounts for bulk purchases, please contact Trilogy Christian Publishing.
Trilogy Disclaimer: The views and content expressed in this book are those of the author and may not necessarily reflect the views and doctrine of Trilogy Christian Publishing or the Trinity Broadcasting Network.
10 9 8 7 6 5 4 3 2 1
Library of Congress Cataloging-in-Publication Data is available.
ISBN 979-8-89597-142-0
ISBN 979-8-89597-143-7 (ebook)

Dedication

My Parents: Deacon Thomas and Deaconess Evangeline Roberson were promoted to heaven in December 2019. They were married for 59 years. We thank them for raising our family in the fear and admiration of the Lord, and for loving us with unconditional love and compassion. They remain deeply loved and deeply missed. Thank you, God, for great parents.

My older sister: Reverend Dr. Mary Winters was promoted to heaven in December 2020, she is entirely cherished and missed. We thank her for being our loving sister. She was married to her surviving husband, Reverend Dr. Virgil for 38 years.

Epigraph

Can We Ask for Anything?

"Marriage Prayer Request"

*God, could You send me a mate
who believes and walks in faith, not fate?*

*Someone that depends solely on You,
and will share life together too.*

*Learning and growing together
in life's good or stormy weather.*

*Someone who gives encouragement and hope
for times when strength is needed to cope*

*Who together will not fail to pray
for direction and order of footsteps day to day?*

*Will be seeking Your (Jesus) plan for our lives,
center of our focused tries.*

*Whether it's a sunshine celebration or during tides
leaning on You, Holy Spirit, for Your guide.*

*Forgiving and loving one another
showing selflessness and giving to each other.*

6/28/24

By Gail Wright

And this is the confidence that we have in him, that, if we ask anything according to his will, he heareth us: And if we know that he hears us, whatsoever we ask, we know that we have the petitions that we desired of him. - 1 John 5:14-15
(New King James Version, NKJV)

Acknowledgements

To My Family

A special thanks to my husband, Richard, whose love, support, and encouragement over the years and while completing this book has been a blessing.

An exceptional thanks and gratitude to my daughter, La'tisha, whose willingness to provide editorial support, substantial revisions, and critical review of this work and previous works has been a great support and a significant contribution to this book.

I am deeply grateful to my sister, Linda, for her support and significant contribution in the completion of this book by helping in the conception of the work, collaborating on it, and her insight in verifying information about our parents.

To my other sisters, Verda and Angeline, who are always there as my encouragers and cheerleaders; thank you with gratitude and appreciation.

I am deeply grateful to my father's baby sister, Aunt Janice, for her assistance in providing information about our grandparents' lives.

I am deeply grateful to my mother's baby sister, Aunt Betty, for authenticating information about our parents and grandparents.

To all other family members and friends who supported me with this book and my previous books, *The Adventures of Alfred: The Greatest Fruit of All, The Adventures of Alfred: Mom I'm Growing Up Now, From the Ditch to The Road, S.J. Strong, and Alfred and Friends: Fun Summer and Afterschool Coloring and Activity Book*—Thank you so much for your support!

Table of Contents

Foreword..13
Preface...15
Introduction....................................17
Prologue..21
Early Life and Background of Thomas and Evangeline..23
Chapter 1: Upbringings........................29
Chapter 2: An Amazing Wedding Day Envisioned!....33
    Marriage Timeline............................34
    Love at First Sight: The Teenage Years...........36
    Newlywed and Family Commitment: Celebrating Victories and Conquering Storms in the Marriage........................40
    Young Adulthood Years.......................41
    Adulthood Years.............................46
    Achieving Aspirations........................48
    Ministry Commitments........................52
    Love Demonstrated and Family Committed........58
    Poem: "You Are to Us".......................62
Chapter 3: Precious Memories 63
    From Thomas and Evangeline's Children..........64
    From Thomas and Evangeline's Sons-in-law (by marriage date).................69
    From Thomas and Evangeline's Grandchildren (by age)........................73

    From Thomas and Evangeline's Surviving Siblings . . 81

    From Thomas and Evangeline's Best Friends 86

    Poem: "A Household Tradition" 93

    Poem: "The Family Tradition:
    Holiday Hometown Countdown" 94

Chapter 4: The Secret Sauce to Thomas and Evangeline's Long Marriage 95

    Hey, Did You Know? 97

    Poem: He & She 99

    Fifty-Ninth Wedding Anniversary Breakdown 100

    Anniversary Breakdown 101

Chapter 5: Life Happenings: Advanced Years 103

    Poems from the Obituaries- "Heaven Bound" 108

    "Going Up Yonder" 109

    Leaving a Family and Spiritual Legacy 111

Chapter 6: Uplifting Marriage Resources 113

    Love and Marriage Verses for Couples 114

    Gratitude For His Faithfulness 116

    Blessings Over the Family 118

    Prayer of Salvation 119

    Encouraging Quotes 120

    Word Search: Attributes of Love & Marriage 1 122

    Word Search: Attributes of Love & Marriage 2 123

Bibliography 125

Foreword

When I hear the name Gail R. Wright, an amazing number of thoughts come to me. Who else can yield to the spirit of God for instruction to write and advocate for our youth of today for all ages with a creative mindset, a pure heart, and a renewed spirit unlike any other writer you can imagine. The Bible tells us in Proverbs 22:29 (NKJV) "Do you see a man who excels in his work? He will stand before kings; He will not stand before unknown men."

As we see an anointed, God-fearing servant, passionate, filled with creative gifts and talents, with the ability to connect as an award-winning poet, an author of five books for children and youth that include activities to help our children (and even my grandchild) to develop their critical thinking and reading ability and skills. We now know her gifts and talents have made much room for her as I am reading *I Do! The Love Story. Until Death Do Us Part.* I believe it will be an award-winning project chronicling the life journeys of my dad and mom, Thomas and Evangeline Roberson.

As she tells the story of their uncertainties, moved with feelings and tears, causing healing and even joy, it proves her authenticity and creative writing skills as she unfolds the stories of mom and dad's life. She shares testimonies of the families' memories.

As an author, clinical counselor, and sister of the author of this book, Gail R. Wright, I have read and used each of her books thus far for my enjoyment, coaching, small-group support, and with self-help work teen girls. Her books have been dynamic tools for my family, my business, programs, and ministry. I know this will be an inspirational read for you as it was for me.

Minister Dr. Linda Jordan

Preface

My name is Gail Wright, an author of children's and youth books and the fourth daughter of five siblings born to our parents, Thomas and Evangeline Roberson, written about in this biography.

The purpose of the book is to provide hope, endurance, commitment, encouragement, and a demonstration of walking with God by faith for those embarking on or experiencing marriage.

This book honors my parents who were committed to marriage for fifty-nine years before they were promoted to heaven in December 2019. This book is to encourage couples, to keep Jesus in the center of their marriage relationship and to allow Him to order their steps.

INTRODUCTION

The heroes of this story had no regrets! Staying married for fifty-nine years is a long-term commitment and should carry with it a wealth of knowledge and wisdom about being in a relationship. This book and story are a narrative biography about a couple's committed marriage and relationship to God, each other, and family. They were utterly in love and in holy matrimony until the end. Together, they served God until the end of their lives, with Thomas being promoted to heaven first in December. Less than a week later, Evangeline joined him on the same day as Thomas' celebration of life, December 19th. This book is their Love Story: *I Do! The Love Story. Until Death Do Us Part*!

This story is being told from me and my sisters' points of view. We share our thoughts of how God preserved their marriage through all those years. It contains my parents' world experiences, beliefs, attitudes, views, and feelings of hopes, fears, faith, and commitments, as well as their way of thinking about the marriage relationship and building a family. This is an interpretation of what we observed through Thomas and Evangeline's lives and the difference they made in their community and their world. The book discusses: holy matrimony, marriage commitment, ministry commitment, relationship with God, precious family memories, life happenings, plus marriage verses, marriage anniversary poems, hey-did-you -know facts, encouraging quotes, uplifting marriage resources, and word search puzzles. A favorite of Thomas and Evangeline. May their family legacy live on.

WORDS FROM MY PARENTS

No matter how much I want to talk about them and their impact on our lives.   I can hear my parents say: "Baby do not talk about us so much…. talk about God… speak of his goodness… do not forget Jesus." So, I will be talking about Jesus and His saving grace in their marriage. His guidance in their lives to live out His purpose for them as a family. And how God sustained their marriage for so many years. They would not ordinarily want a book written about them, but for His glory they would that God be given the praise through it. This book tells their story for His glory.

INTRODUCTION

~ Bless Our Home ~

Trust in the LORD with all your heart and lean not on your own understanding ⁶ in all your ways submit to him and he will make your paths straight.

**- Proverbs 3:5-6
(New International Version, NIV)**

Prologue

BRIEF FAMILY HISTORY AND CULTURAL BACKGROUND

Evangeline's mother, Annie V. Hines was born in May 1909 in Martin County, Williamston, North Carolina. Her younger daughter, Betty, shares that her mother worked for a doctor; and for as long as she and Evangeline could remember, their mother, had been in a wheelchair. Annie V. had one brother. She died in May 1971 at the age of 62. Evangeline's grandfather was (Richard) Richmond Hines. A farm laborer, he was born in October 1877 in Martin County, North Carolina, and died in February 1919. Evangeline's maternal grandmother was Mary Everett.

Evangeline's father, James Henry, was born in 1907 to Annie Purvis in North Carolina. His father, William H. Williams, was born in 1879, and resided in Nashville, North Carolina. He passed away in 1947 at the age of sixty-eight. They were married in 1905.

James Henry worked as a sharecropper and a farm laborer and had several siblings. According to Evangeline's younger sister, Betty, their father died in 1956 when she was at the tender age of 11 years old, and Evangeline was 13 years old. He passed away on Betty's birthday that

October. James and Annie V. had several children together. They were married in 1923.

Thomas' father James Edward Roberson, Sr. and his mother, Mary Gladys were born two years apart: James Edward in February 1910 in Pitts County, North Carolina, and Mary Gladys in July 1912 in Martin County, North Carolina. They had several children. His parents were sharecroppers on a farm. According to their youngest daughter, Janice, her parents had limited education. James Sr. was only able to attend elementary school. Mary Gladys was only able to go to school up to the eighth grade. Although she successfully completed her eighth-grade year, she was not able to continue because the walk to the new school for ninth grade was too far. James Edward and Mary Gladys celebrated their 50th Anniversary in November of 1981. Not long after, James Edward passed away in January 1982. Mary Gladys would go on to live nearly another 10 years before being laid to rest in March 1991.

Mary Gladys' mother was Aurelia "Relia" Williams, and her father was Cain Williams. Cain was born in May 1875. Relia was born in Aug 1879. Cain passed in January 1942 and was survived by Relia until she passed in May 1944.

Thomas' great grandparents and his mother, Mary Gladys' grandparents were Shade Williams, Sr. (born in 1839) and Leah Williams (born in 1842). Leah passed in

PROLOGUE

1910 at the age of 68 and Shade passed in 1915 at the age of 75, two months before his 76th birthday. Thomas's paternal grandparents were Smith and Dorothy "Doras" Perkins Roberson. Smith was born in 1871 and passed away in December 1936. Doras was born in 1877 and died in December 1945. Thomas's paternal great grandparents were Jesse and Mandy Roberson.

Some of the family history and cultural background information: dates and names were researched using Ancestry Online sources. Other information was provided by surviving members of the family.

EARLY LIFE AND BACKGROUND OF THOMAS AND EVANGELINE
Birth, Birthplace, Childhood, and Juvenile Years

Thomas and Evangeline's nationality was American. Their ethnicity/ culture, African American. Thomas was born in 1941 in Williamston, North Carolina to James Edward Roberson, Sr., and Mary Gladys (Williams) Roberson. Evangeline was born in 1943 to James Henry Williams and Annie V. (Hines)Williams in Everett, North Carolina.

Thomas went to school up to the fifth grade and later went back to school to complete his diploma at J.R. Tucker High School in 1993. Evangeline went to Everett High School in Robersonville, North Carolina until the 11th grade. Thomas started farming when he was a young boy.

Evangeline worked in the home most of the time to help the family, but occasionally would help on the farm, too.

Evangeline and her mom

PROLOGUE

Thomas' dad and mother

A BIBLE MARRIAGE LOVE STORY: THE CREATION OF ADAM AND EVE

Adam

Genesis 1:27-28 (NIV) So God created man in His own image; in the image of God, He created him; male and female He created them. God blessed them and said to them, "Be fruitful and increase in number; fill the earth and subdue it. Rule over the fish in the sea and the birds in the sky and over every living creature that moves on the ground."

Life in God's Garden

Genesis: 2:7-8 (NKJV): "And the Lord God formed a man from the dust of the ground and breathed into his nostrils the breath of life, and the man became a living being. The LORD God planted a garden eastward in Eden, and there He put the man whom He had formed."

Eve

Genesis 2:18 (NKJV): "And the LORD God said, "It is not good that man should be alone; I will make him a helper comparable to him."

Genesis 2:21-23 (NKJV) And the LORD God caused a deep sleep to fall on Adam, and he slept; and He took one of his ribs and closed up the flesh in its place. Then the rib which the LORD God had taken from man He made into a woman, and He brought her to the man. And Adam said: "This is now bone of my bones, And flesh of my flesh; She shall be called Woman, Because she was taken out of Man."

Jesus Is Our Standard For Marriage!

The Bible says: The church is the bride of Christ, Jesus' bridegroom, and Christ is the head of the church. As believers, Christ should also be the center of our marriage, Christ, husband, wife, then children. The husband should love the wife as Christ loves the church and the wife should respect her husband in the union of marriage. God will lead, guide, and direct the family. This leaves no room for selfishness but encourages selflessness in marriage. Christ is our standard and shows the husbands and wives how they ought to live their lives by showing their love for each other.

Let Us Follow Jesus' Example

Ephesians 5:22-25 (NKJV) "Wives, submit to your own husbands, as to the Lord. For the husband is head of the wife, as also Christ is head of the church; and He is the Savior of the body. Therefore, just as the church is subject to Christ, so let the wives be to their own husbands in everything. Husbands, love your wives, just as Christ also loved the church and gave Himself for her."

CHAPTER 1
UPBRINGINGS

Thomas and Evangeline's upbringing was similar to living in a house where love was demonstrated. They both had a large family with multiple siblings. Thomas grew up with both of his parents in the household from childhood through adulthood. However, Evangeline didn't grow up with her father in the household during the earlier part of her teenage years, because of his death when she was thirteen. Her mother did not remarry. She, her mother, and her siblings stepped up and assumed responsibilities of the household obligations to help hold the family together.

They both followed the rules of their parents' households while living in the home. Those household rules may have differed based on each home. Thomas and Evangeline, families lived on a farmland and worked on a farm. Their relationship with family members – in both homes - was said to be a tightly-knitted one. They helped each other out when there was a need. Both families also attended a church. They were known to have had similar activities for fun like getting together for cookouts and other family activities.

Thomas revealed when he was young that his hobbies were playing games and hanging out with his siblings. However, when he got older he had a passion for making things like furniture, reupholstering, and building additions to the house. He also enjoyed reading and studying the Bible and watching ministries on television. Fun fact: His other hobbies involved watching nature shows and Westerns (cowboy movies and TV shows), as he got older. He also loved to purchase new electronics to expand his knowledge. And he loved buying cars, especially fine large ones, since he was a tall man.

"Evangeline had a passion and hobby in her earlier years to make many beautiful creative things" says her baby sister, Betty. As she grew up she developed an interest in sewing all types of things like curtains, clothes, comforters, chairs and sofas, and stool cushions. Fun fact: Her hobbies also included gardening, relaxing while watching Hallmark Christmas family shows, and solving puzzles. Her other passion was calling family members and friends to check on them and pray for them, when necessary. Evangeline enjoyed dressing up in her church outfits with beautiful accessories and hats. She also loved to cook for the family. Their plans and goals centered around serving God, family, and others. They desired to live life on purpose by doing God's plan for their lives.

UPBRINGINGS

Many are the plans in a person's heart, but it is the LORD's purpose that prevails.
Proverbs 19:21 (NIV)

CHAPTER 2
AN AMAZING WEDDING DAY ENVISIONED!

Oh, the beauty of a man and a woman joining together in holy matrimony. Envision, a traditional wedding happening. You enter the venue on that special day to celebrate the momentous occasion with the couple. The music is tastefully playing, setting the atmosphere in the room to tranquility. The scenery is decorated stunningly with blossoming flowers, magnificently designed bows, and scented candles, positioned with precision, intention, and care around the venue. The wedding parties are present, and all pause as the expectancy of the bride appearing in the room increases. As the door opens, sounds of awe and expressions of joyfulness and tears sweep the room.

The bride elegantly walks down the aisle to her man, the love of her life. He stands waiting to join hands with his woman, the love of his life. They are ready to commit

I DO! THE LOVE STORY

to marriage through their vows to one another and to God. They are about to share their lives and God's plan for their lives, together.

"For Better or for Worse, for Richer or for Poorer, in Sickness and in Health, to Love and to Cherish, Til Death Do Us Part." Marital vows are asked of each of them. I DO! – is their response. Their new life and journey together as one begins.

> *But at the beginning of creation God 'made them male and female." For this reason a man will leave his father and mother and be united to his wife, and the two will become one flesh." So, they are no longer two, but one flesh. Therefore what God has joined together, let no one separate.*
>
> **Mark 10:6-9 (NIV)**

MARRIAGE TIMELINE

BEGINNING OF MARRIAGE:
November 1960
Thomas, 19 yrs old
Evangeline, 17 yrs old

FIRST 10 YEARS
Tin November 1970
Thomas, 29 yrs old
Evangeline, 27 yrs old

FIRST YEAR
Paper November 1961
Newlyweds

(20) YEARS
Silver November 1980
Thomas, 39 yrs old
Evangeline, 37 yrs old

34

AN AMAZING WEDDING DAY ENVISIONED!

Fun Facts About the 59th Wedding Anniversary
59th Anniversary is called: Mink's Wedding

- The traditional gift for this wedding anniversary is typically lace, symbolizing the beautiful intricacy and elegant detail of your many years together.
- Modern gift: Marble
- Flower: White Rose: sincerity, virtue, everlasting love
- Sapphire jewelry- Sapphire is the traditional gemstone for the wedding anniversary just short of sixty years, symbolizing wisdom, faithfulness, and steadfast love.

Nevertheless let each one of you in particular so love his own wife as himself, and let the wife see that she respects her husband.

- Ephesians 5:33 (NKJV)

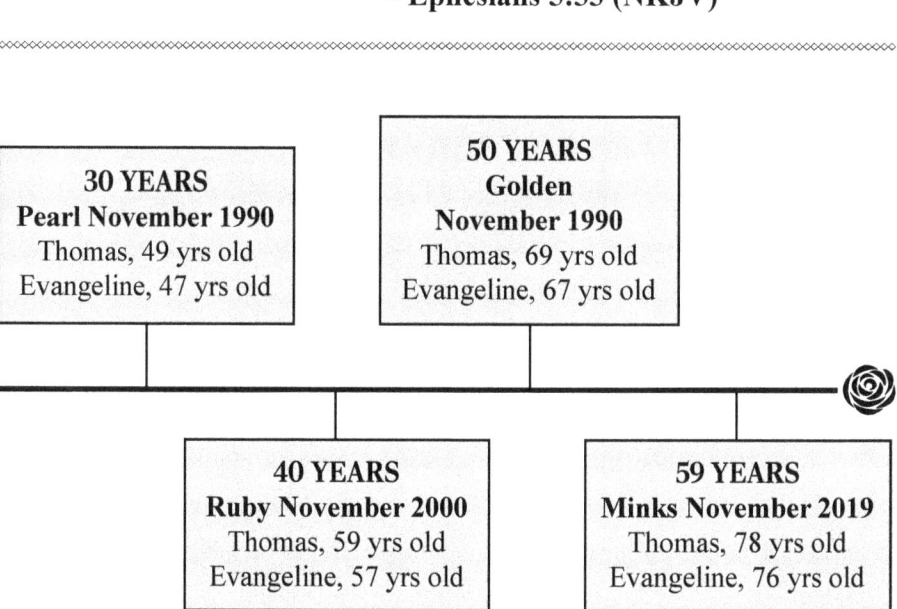

---

30 YEARS
Pearl November 1990
Thomas, 49 yrs old
Evangeline, 47 yrs old

50 YEARS
Golden
November 1990
Thomas, 69 yrs old
Evangeline, 67 yrs old

40 YEARS
Ruby November 2000
Thomas, 59 yrs old
Evangeline, 57 yrs old

59 YEARS
Minks November 2019
Thomas, 78 yrs old
Evangeline, 76 yrs old

Thomas (19) and Evangeline (17)

LOVE AT FIRST SIGHT: THE TEENAGE YEARS

How did the lovely couple meet? Thomas tells the story of how he was introduced to Evangeline by one of his brothers who was already courting one of Evangeline's older sisters. He thought she was pretty. She was young, with caramel-toned skin; and she was petite, with bright, light brown eyes that seemed to sparkle when she talked. He was a handsome teenaged boy with ebony skin, and a tall, athletic build, , with kind, yet bold dark brown eyes.

Evangeline's baby sister, Betty, says when Evangeline met Thomas, she told her that she liked him. Betty asked her, "Have you told Mom and Dad?"

Alice, their older sister who was dating Thomas' brother chimed in, "Thomas likes you, too. He talks about you all the time."

According to Betty, soon after that Thomas started courting Evangeline. Courting. that's what they called dating in those days. Thomas would pull up in his car with a big pretty smile on his face and Betty would start in.

Evangeline asked, "Who is that outside'?"

Betty answered, "It's your friend out there."

Evangeline excitedly said, "Go to the door! Go to the door! I gotta get ready."

Betty would go to the door and Thomas would always ask, "Is Evangeline here?"

Betty would respond. "Who are you?"

"I'm Evangeline's friend. Can you get her for me?" Thomas, who had driven up in their back driveway where cars that came to the house would usually park, would ask.

Evangeline would finally yell, "He can come in!"

According to Evangeline's sister, Betty, they always kept their house spotless because their mom was sick, and they couldn't have germs around. When Thomas came in the first time, their mom rolled her wheelchair into the living room to talk to him.

Thomas whispered to Betty. "Is this your mother?"

Evangeline answered, "Yes."

Thomas looked at Mrs. Annie V. and stated his position. "Ma'am, I like your daughter, and I would like to date her."

Betty says she thought to herself, *you don't find guys these days that meet a parent and ask that question.* As time went by, their mom really liked him.

Thomas and Evangeline started to date and learned about each other's likes, wishes, dislikes, hopes, and dreams for the future. They were opposites in personalities like fire and ice. Nevertheless, they were extremely interested in each other. Thomas' disposition was calm. His sanguine, choleric, and phlegmatic-these temperament descriptions meant his personality was peaceful, laidback, but confident and firm. He loved the color yellow and always dressed in fine apparel. He was also very polite, an extrovert who loved to serve people in large settings.

Evangeline often talked to her children about Thomas' ways. She'd say how some of his attributes contributed to her attraction to him while they were dating. He was an extrovert and Evangeline's disposition was energetic, strong, and committed. Her distinct personality was reflective of a choleric and melancholy temperament. Her focus, organization, and creative abilities were some of the traits that piqued Thomas' interest in her. She was an introvert, who loved to invite small groups of people to the house to fellowship with.

Because she was an introvert, unlike him, they did not always take pleasure in the same things. However, they adapted and learned as they grew together that they had some similar interests: going to church, family gatherings like cookouts and holiday dinners, shopping at certain stores, eating foods like cabbage, barbeque, and chicken; and going to the park, and sitting in nature, making creative things, and taking trips together with friends and family.

After courting, they fell in love and began their journey. It's said there was no engagement. Thomas proposed to Evangeline, and she said "yes!" Evangeline shared with her children that her mother gave permission for her to be married by signing a consent to marry form, since she was only 17 years old, and Thomas was 19. In late November, they got married. They had a beautiful baby girl the month before in October.

It was not a traditional wedding as we know it today and as was envisioned earlier in this chapter. She did not have the traditional wedding with something old, something new, something borrowed or something blue. Her hair was not combed in any fancy style. There were no bridesmaids nor groomsmen. She did not wear anything fancy, only plain clothes. A picture of Evangeline and Thomas shows her combed hair going toward the back of her head with a hair pen or bow holding it together. No fancy venue was decorated or rented for the occasion. No wedding impressions, wedding songs sung, or wedding pamphlet. There was no grand gathering afterwards to celebrate the special occasion. The story goes: they recited their vows with witnesses, one being one of her sisters at a minister's home somewhere in the countryside of North Carolina. Thomas said his wedding vows first and Evangeline followed. And when asked by the children who kissed who first, Evangeline said that she kissed him first. They always told their children that they believed marriage takes three: God, man, and woman.

NEWLYWED AND FAMILY COMMITMENT: CELEBRATING VICTORIES AND CONQUERING STORMS IN THE MARRIAGE

The newlyweds' faces shined radiantly like the sunshine in the sky. Filled with expectation and joy, they are ready for their new faith walk together. They trusted God for His plan for their lives as He orders their steps through each milestone in their marriage. Like all couples starting a new adventure together, they have new victories and challenges ahead but are glad to grow in life together. They had seen and heard how God was faithful, made a way and worked things out in their parents' lives. They were believing for wonderful things to happen on their new faith journey.

YOUNG ADULTHOOD YEARS

The next momentous milestone in their life: creating a family. They wanted a nice-sized family, but maybe not as big as their parents' family. For a while, they lived in North Carolina where he worked to provide for his new family; which then included two beautiful baby girls born in the first two years of marriage; one in 1960 and the other in 1961. A year later, in 1962, they were expecting another precious little one. But in a heartbreaking turn of events, the new baby, a boy, was stillborn. It was a challenging time for the family, especially for parents who were only 19 and 21. Walking through grief during the traumatic loss was difficult. Nevertheless, God was with them and helped them through it. To honor their love for their son and his presence in the world, although only for a moment, they named the baby boy and wrote his name in a Bible. Sadly, we couldn't locate the Bible to note his name.

God had not forgotten their desire for more children. A year later in 1963, they were expecting a baby again. This time, another beautiful baby girl. The deeply-in-love couple became a beautiful, blessed family of five living in Carolina, in a house near Thomas' parents in the countryside. But they wanted to expand again. This time, to another state.

A new milestone was reached: the family of five moved to Richmond, Virginia in hopes of providing a better opportunity for themselves. They had been prayerful about the move and acted by faith on what they felt God was leading them to do. It's not known how difficult this move was; they were leaving most of their family and the place where they grew up, North Carolina, and going to uncharted territory. They understood they would miss seeing their loved ones every day, but for sure felt it was the right move. They believed the opportunity they were searching for could be found in Virginia.

It was a humble beginning; but this small start didn't stop their dream of providing the best for their family. They strived to reach their American dream. For them that included two priorities: First, having a Christ-centered marriage, home, and family through serving God. Second, being providers, working hard, teaching their children how to trust God, practice family values, develop dreams, and accomplish goals. Thomas and Evangeline believed God was the source of their happiness and that even though He gave them resources: jobs, finances, houses, cars, health and more, He did not want them to depend on things for security or to pursue things instead of pursuing Him, the Creator. God wanted them to trust Him for their wants and needs.

AN AMAZING WEDDING DAY ENVISIONED!

Then an amazing thing happened. After moving to Richmond, they were blessed with another beautiful baby girl, born in 1964. By this time, Thomas was twenty-three years old, and Evangeline was twenty-one. The young parents were so pleased to have had four active, beautiful little girls because both wanted children they could grow up with. Once they finally made their transition to Richmond, they lived in a house with Evangeline's sister, Betty, and her brother-in-law. They lived with them for a short time while looking for an apartment. Before long, they found their first apartment in 1964 on Carmine Street in the Church Hill neighborhood of Richmond. Later, in 1967, they lived on Ambrose Street on the Eastend of Richmond.

Evangeline at the apartment

Later in 1972 they moved from Church Hill to a two-story house on Jefferson Davis Highway in South Richmond.

They were still desiring and believing for something more. What they really wanted was to own a home in the rural area in the countryside of Richmond. And they did.

Yet, another momentous thing happened. God heard the couple's desires and answered their prayer. The family moved to a house in rural Charles City, VA in 1972. The family of six lived and grew up in their Charles City home; then excitedly had one more beautiful bundle of joy, a baby girl in 1973. God blessed them with a total of five lovely little girls. The older children were each one year apart, and the last child nine years apart from the fourth child. Now they had a lovely family of seven. And for the rest of the little Roberson girls' childhood, Thomas and Evangeline nurtured them to grow individually into the unique person God made them to be. They also developed their faith and relationship in God.

The Roberson girls experienced some awesome childhood moments growing up together, running, playing, and enjoying being a kid. However, it wasn't without some growing pains. Those adorable daddy's girls weren't perfect kids, but adolescents (and later teenagers) with their own personalities and thoughts. They were mainly obedient, but like most teenagers needed to be reminded of some rules at times. For example: Like what time to come home. When asked about following the Roberson family rules, one of the children, recalls how they had to be in the house by 12:00, how they couldn't look at certain television shows, and how they could only listen to Christian music. They also recalled how they weren't able to stay at anyone's home unless their parents knew the family, even though they were older teenagers. Like most teenagers, they weren't fond of these rules.

During their adolescent years, each child dealt with their emotions and decision making as they grew and became young adults. Each dealing with that familiar development phase: *I'm Grown Now! Or I'm Growing Up Now!* The Roberson girls also dealt with growing pains. One of the siblings shared that it wasn't that they didn't think their parents knew what they were talking about; but they did think that things had changed some. Thomas and Evangeline's children agree that as young children they thought their parents knew everything and could do anything. We also agree that something does happen when one becomes a teenager. The enemy gives thoughts to kids at an incredibly young age and during the teenage years. The enemy puts a suggestion (thought) in a young person's mind. He distorts and increases the teenage mindset that they know everything, and their parents don't what them to have fun. This can cause rebellion against the family and create conflict in the home. The Roberson girls were careful of this deception and took their parents advice about things.

There were times when Thomas and Evangeline's children didn't understand the why or the why not of certain things, nor did they agree with all their parents' choices growing up, but they later understood why it was so important to trust their parents' decisions and guidance. God had placed their parents over them to shield them from harm. As the children grew up they realized that their parents were wise in their dealings. Thomas and Evangeline sought Godly wisdom to direct and teach them right from wrong. As the household grew daily, and the girls experienced their teenage years it created multiple teachable moments for the whole family. Every generation discovers new things and evolves, yet they shouldn't discount the previous generations' knowledge and wisdom.

ADULTHOOD YEARS

As the years went by, several turns of events changed their lives and drew them closer to God. Marriage is not always a bed of roses, as you might have heard people say. Thomas and Evangeline, like any couple, might have had agreements, disagreements, and heated discussions about topics because there were thoughts from different points

AN AMAZING WEDDING DAY ENVISIONED!

of view. However, that didn't change their desire to remain committed to each other when they had challenges. There were situations they were aware of before marriage and some challenges they endured after being married. Nevertheless, they sought God about how they should deal with each event as a family. A persistent life challenge for the family was Evangeline's unstable health. She was sick often and spent many days hospitalized for a variety of illnesses. In her youth, she experienced many traumatic events. Losing her father at the gentle age of thirteen, seeing her mother become wheelchair-bound after numerous strokes, and later losing one of her sisters to liver disease. This all could have been a life disadvantage for her. However, that was not the case. Evangeline prayerfully dealt with every heartache and pain, and God gave her strength to get through them. God graced her with favor as she walked through her challenges and trusted Him.

She was an extraordinarily strong individual and determined to rise above her circumstances with faith in God and with the support of her husband, family, and friends. As a family, Thomas and Evangeline prayed and confessed her healing as a believer and overcomer over sickness, disease, and grief. She endured in her commitment to her family to be the best version of herself she could be with God's help. Her husband and children believed that she was truly a Proverbs 31 woman because of the way she lived. She believed and would always say, nothing was impossible for her through God and He would give her strength.

After the move to Richmond, one of Thomas' dear brothers passed away during a visit home from the military.

They were very close. Again, God carried them through. There were numerous losses of family and friends as the years went by; nevertheless, goodness and mercy followed them all the days of their lives as they leaned on God for strength.

> *I will love You, O Lord, my strength.* [2] *The Lord is my rock and my fortress and my deliverer; My God, my strength, in whom I will trust; My shield and the horn of my salvation, my stronghold.*
>
> **Psalm 18: 1-2 (KJV)**

ACHIEVING ASPIRATIONS

Although he was remarkably busy working and raising a family, Thomas had an important personal goal he wanted to achieve. After many years of being out of school, he decided to go back to earn his high school diploma. This was a tremendous undertaking for his growing family to witness. They wanted to set an example for their children about achieving goals and never giving up. And they wanted their children to be high achievers to change their lives for the better, while also getting involved in church ministry and allowing God to use them as they sought Him.

AN AMAZING WEDDING DAY ENVISIONED!

Thomas receiving his high school diploma

Thomas worked two jobs when necessary to provide for the family. As a Richmond resident, he maintained a career in production, manufacturing, and commercial driving for over 25 years at Crawford Manufacturing, Carisbrook Industries, and Caraustar. The children watched with amazement as their parents used their many skills. Evangeline worked at the same factory as Thomas.

She took opportunities as a seamstress to do piecework to make extra money. She later operated a home business as a seamstress, and for many years she blessed others with her gifts and talents. She designed and stitched bedding, curtains, clothes such as dresses, suits, scarves, and even upholstered furniture. And she had a green thumb with plants and gardening.

Picture mom with Tish and her flowers.

The couple's combined hard work and special talents caused others to believe they were affluent when really they were just wealthy in God's favor and blessings! They were grateful and thankful for how God always provided for the family.

Thomas and Evangeline were never able to attend college, but they encouraged their children to go to college, university, or trade school to further their education and create better opportunities for themselves. God continued answering Thomas and Evangeline's prayers and blessed their seed (children) to do just that. Each of the Roberson girls graduated from high school and went to college. Some of them received associates, bachelor, master, and doctoral degrees across different fields of study. They've worked in public service, local and state government, private industry, and ministry. They've owned businesses in private Christian education, a cosmetology school, and beauty spa. They've been authors, teachers, counselors, and interior designers. Over the years, Thomas and Evangeline were able to experience their children's and even their grandchildren's celebrations and accomplishments because of God's many favors and blessings. Some of the grandchildren also went on to complete varying degrees; and some followed in the business ownership and cross-sector work environment as those before them.

Thomas and Evangeline celebrated achievements and victories on a continuous basis seeing God's goodness and faithfulness. They lived surrendered to Christ. They wanted divine guidance for their lives, so they surrendered their will and direction to God. Even when times were rough, they trusted God, obeyed Him, and respected His timing. They understood that His grace was sufficient to keep them in their marriage and ministry during good and difficult times. They lived a blessed life despite the challenges because God was with them.

And still, the elephant in the room of those challenges was a family history of sickness, diseases, and poverty. The family came against each and declared the blessing of God over the cycles of sicknesses, babies out of wedlock, miscarriages, endometriosis, stomach ulcers, diabetes, high blood pressure, cholesterol, heart disease, cancer, dementia, and strokes. Jesus is bigger than any sickness. We continue to denounce all manners of illness and instead declare and decree victory over it to rewrite this part of the family story and break the generational curse in these areas. We cancel these things out of every generation in the name of Jesus. Jesus has already paid the price. Isaiah 53:5 (NKJV) says, "But He was wounded for our transgressions, He was bruised for our iniquities; The chastisement for our peace was upon Him, And by His stripes we are healed." First Peter 2:24 (NKJV) supports the Word in Isaiah, in this matter, "who Himself bore our sins in His own body on the tree, that we, having died to sins, might live for righteousness—by whose stripes you were healed." And the family receives it. Praise God!

MINISTRY COMMITMENTS

Thomas and Evangeline were a married couple of faith and individually committed to the ministry to be used by God to do His will. God began to change their lives for His service even more as they continued to surrender and be committed to Him. They desired to be led by the Holy Spirit, so they prayed and sought God about their service to

Him. They didn't let their feelings or emotions lead them. Connecting with the right ministry was essential. They felt called to the ministry of deacon and deaconess.

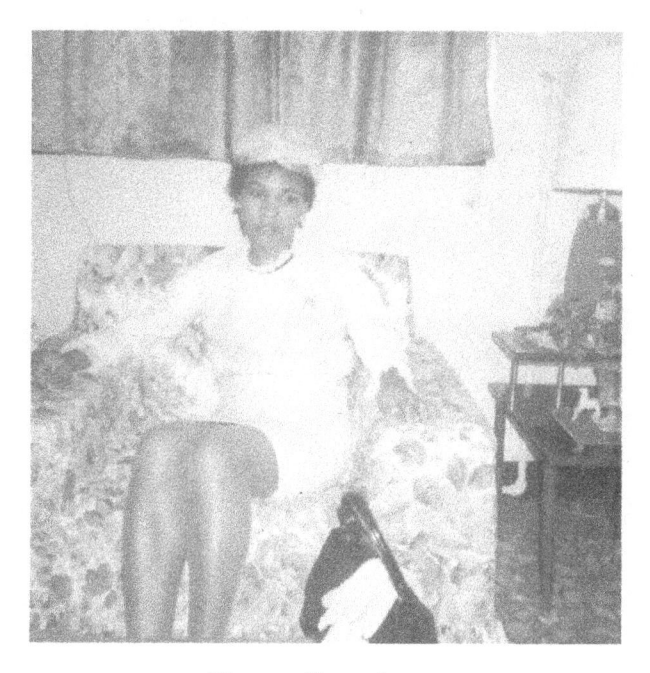

Evangeline picture

Thomas picture

They served in the deacon and deaconess ministry office. They took their children to church with them every time they served. The children spent many days, afternoons, and sometimes nights, hanging out at the church while their parents went to meetings, served at functions, in church services, and at community events. There were no children's ministries during this time. When the children were old enough to participate in ministry, they joined the church's usher board, choir, helped their parents and generally served where needed. Thomas and Evangeline felt this was good because they were serving in the church while learning about commitment and dedication to ministry and to God. Each of their daughters was establishing their own personal walk with Him. And as time went on, after being taught the Word, hearing the Word, learning the Word, and doing what the Word admonishes, each child accepted Jesus as their personal Savior.

Thomas and Evangeline ensured that their children prayed as a family, read the Word as a family, and went to church as a family. They would always tell their children to pray and seek God about any situation before acting on it. But like any child, there were some hard lessons to learn when they didn't do what they knew as right. Thomas and Evangeline had a relationship and commitment to God, not religion or a denomination, and their lives reflected it. Thomas became a deacon at the early age of thirty and at the end of his life he was also a chaplain. He was a faithful member of his church demonstrating his passion for Christ and for the people of the community by serving as a deacon for 49 years. Additionally, he served several years on the church's stewardship committee and new members board.

Evangeline served for 49 years, in later years as a deaconess-emeritus who visited the sick, supported candidates for baptism, served Holy Communion, and assisted with outreach when she was able. She was creative, enthusiastic, strong, and diligent in her service not only to the church and community, but to her family. They were both very committed to ministry and their lives were filled with the faith walk and the fruit of the Spirit.

Deacons likewise must be men worthy of respect [honorable, financially ethical, of good character], not double-tongued [speakers of half-truths], not addicted to wine, not greedy for dishonest gain, ⁹ but upholding and fully understanding the mystery [that is, the true doctrine] of the [Christian] faith with a clear conscience [resulting from behavior consistent with spiritual maturity]. ¹⁰ These men must first be tested; then if they are found to be blameless and beyond reproach [in their Christian lives], let them serve as deacons. ¹¹ Women must likewise be worthy of respect, not malicious gossips, but self-controlled, [thoroughly] trustworthy in all things.

1 Timothy 3:8-11 (Amplified, AMP)

AN AMAZING WEDDING DAY ENVISIONED!

"OUR HEROES"

Dad and mom, you are our heroes
imparting in us your love

Godly wisdom and knowledge
Striving to keep us from life's billow
that we will not hit ground zero

You fill us with the word of God
and if necessary, did not spare the rod

Because you had God
we did not stray too far apart

Love,
Your daughters and sons-in-law

Forty-third Anniversary

Thomas 62 years old and Evangeline 60 years old

2003

By Gail Wright

LOVE DEMONSTRATED AND FAMILY COMMITTED

Thomas and Evangeline decided that they would trust God and walk by faith. They believed that God is faithful to do what He promised. They knew there was no such thing as a perfect life in the way that the world defines perfect, but they desired to live Gods perfect plan and will for their lives. And that is the perfect life. They demonstrated love for God, one another in marriage, family, friends, and others in relationships.

In their marriage, they demonstrated love by "The Fruit of the Spirit" beginning with showing love for one another, showing kindness, patience, longsuffering, peace in the home, self-control, care for one another, and sharing with one another joy, goodness, selflessness, and faithfulness. They had their marriage differences and challenges through the years, but they hung in there. They trusted in a purpose bigger than themselves. Practicing these spiritual fruits was a daily walk. Sometimes they had to remind each other of their purpose, that they were on the right team, and that they could do all things through Christ who strengthens them.

As a family, Thomas and Evangeline demonstrated love by spending quality time with the children. They would go to places everyone enjoyed like the park for recreation and take trips to see family and friends. They showed their children and grandchildren, by instructions and examples, how to be disciples of Christ. They could have taught their girls about any religion, belief, or set of morals; but they chose to teach them about the One they learned to trust and love, the biblical Jesus. As spouses, they enjoyed each other's companionship and dedicated time for each other. They allowed their children to see their love for one another.

As believers of Christ, they showed the love of God in their everyday walk and talk as they spoke of God's goodness and faithfulness to their children and others they met and knew.

As ambassadors for Christ, and disciples for Christ they loved God, themselves, and others because they believed the Bible, and knew that God loved them. So, as disciples of Jesus, they would go into communities to serve others with the love and compassion received from God. Thomas and Evangeline were known to show selflessness by helping family and others when there was a need, often assisting and putting the needs of others before their own.

As a family serving God, when they were unable to go to church because Evangeline was ill (or something else happened), Thomas and Evangeline conducted Bible study at home. All the children took part, singing, reading, and asking and answering Bible questions as well as praying. According to the girls, there were times when any one of them would fall asleep during Bible study reading. Their parents or their siblings would nudge them awake, then have them to read to keep them engaged. It was important to Thomas and Evangeline to raise the children in a home that loved and served God, and so they did. There was so much love given to each Roberson girl that every child felt like they were the favorite. The parents knew each child's heart and loved them in the special way they needed. Their love for each of their girls showed on a daily basis.

> *So then, as we have opportunity, let us work that which is good toward all men, and especially toward them that are of the household of the faith.*
>
> **- Galatians 6:10 (ESV)**

> *....but as for me and my house, we will serve the Lord.*
>
> **- Joshua 24:15 (Amplified Version, AMP)**

AN AMAZING WEDDING DAY ENVISIONED!

Family group picture

"YOU ARE TO US"

Our mentor
Hero
Encourager
Supporter
Inspiration
Counselor
Role model

You are God's gift to us, and we thank you for

Imparting into us great wisdom
Being so patient
Loving us unconditionally
Being so compassionate
Teaching us Godly principles

We Love You Both Very Much

Your daughters, sons-in-law and grandchildren
Forty-seventh Anniversary
Thomas 66 years old and Evangeline 64 years old

11/21/07
By Gail Wright

CHAPTER 3
Precious Memories

Memories are for keeps! What a great day when you can remember a precious memory about a loved one that makes you smile, laugh, or even cry with joy. Going down memory lane reflecting on the many blessings of God that showed up through our parents' lives was meaningful.

These are just a few pleasant family memories of Thomas and Evangeline. Memories shared by their surviving children, sons-in-law, grandchildren, surviving siblings, and friends. It is the hope of the family that these memories bring the book to life and allows the reader to feel the love given by Thomas and Evangeline, in their acts of kindness and expressions. As the memories heal and bless the ones who wrote the memories, it is hoped that they encourage and bless others.

Roberson Girls group picture

FROM THOMAS AND EVANGELINE'S CHILDREN

Second Daughter, Linda

"I admired how mom always took care of my father's feet. She would say, 'you should take care of your husband.' She would talk about when dad came home from working hard, sometimes his feet were smelly, so she'd put his feet in some water. I watched her do that for my daddy. I was a teenager then. My takeaway was to take care of your husband. That was really amazing. It allowed me to know who she was as a Christian woman. She didn't mind doing it.

"Mom had a routine schedule with housekeeping during the summertime. She would have us do spring/summer cleaning in the home. It taught me good housekeeping habits and good rules to go by. I made my own rules when I left home but still followed some of her guidelines.

"One of Dad's favorite verses, was Proverbs 3:5-6. He loved it so much that he put it as the voicemail on his phone. I remember Daddy saying this scripture. "Trust in the LORD with all thine heart; and lean not unto thine own understanding. In all thy ways acknowledge him, and he shall direct thy paths.

"Dad would always do a wellness check about our salvation and ask how everything is going. He wanted to see where our hearts were. He would ask, 'You love the Lord?' He wanted to make sure our choice was that of the Lord. He had a way of doing it with love. But we knew why he was asking!

"My daddy loved to tell stories. It was storytelling time, and we were sitting around daddy on the living room floor. He started telling us stories about the lady who got a ham thrown through a window because she said the devil might have brought it, but really the Lord sent it. Another story Dad told talked about all the animals that helped the pig jump over the fence so that the pig got home that night. He always knew how to make us laugh."

Third Daughter, Verda

"One of my favorite childhood moments with Dad and Mom was when we did Bible study as a family. They would read and ask us questions, but as we got older Dad would allow us to choose our own chapter to read and explain. They made it fun, by allowing us to lie down on the floor with our pillows to help us enjoy reading the Word. I remember them teaching us the Lord's Prayer and the Ten Commandments.

"I remember when mom taught me how to cook. One of the hardest things was cooking rice and gravy. I couldn't get it right for anything in the world! I had to throw food out several times before I got it right. My mother said 'Faye, that's the easiest thing to cook.' I finally got it, and she was so proud of me. Mom told my older sister to continue to teach me how to cook other foods and I really started cooking more once my older sisters left home. And I've been cooking ever since. I was about twelve or thirteen years old when I really started to master cooking. Now I can cook anything I put my mind to.

"This is one of the scriptures I remember from Dad during childhood, and it stayed in my heart. The Amplified

Version of Matthew 7:21: "Not everyone who says to Me, 'Lord, Lord,' will enter the kingdom of heaven, but only he who does the will of My Father who is in heaven.

"I tried to live my life for God. I wanted to make sure that I entered the kingdom of heaven. I also found out that because I accepted Christ as my personal Savior, I would enter the kingdom of heaven. Praise God!"

Fourth Daughter, The Knee Baby, Gail

"I remember the days when I would come over to my parents' house and I would sit down with Mom and Dad to look at movies and talk for hours. Sometimes I'd be over so long that both of them would fall asleep in their comfortable recliners, and I would too! And when it was time for me to go, they would say 'you don't have to go. Stay a little while.' It was always hard to leave because I enjoyed just hanging around them.

"We would have holiday dinners at Mom and Dad's house. Mom would cook some food and the rest of us would bring covered dishes of all sorts of sides and desserts. There was always enough for everyone to eat and even to take leftovers for the next few days. We had so much fun laughing, talking, reminiscing about other great times together, watching movies, taking pictures, and laying back relaxing. We also enjoyed playing jokes by sneaking photos of the family members sleeping or snoring with their head dropping forward or leaning way to the back or side after eating. Then we let them see it when they woke up. They would say something like I didn't go to sleep! or I wasn't snoring! or I wasn't snoring loud! and then we would laugh and show them the pictures and videos. And they would laugh too because they got caught.

"My sisters and other family members would sing when we got together at my Dad and Mom's house. Sometimes they would sit there listening to us with a smile. Other times they would join in and sing with us if they were familiar with the songs; and sometimes they would even request a song for us to sing. We had so much fun singing and praising the Lord. My father would even surprise us sometimes and come to our engagements to see us. Ministry in Song was our family group name for many years. We were always so happy to see him there."

The Baby Girl, Angie

"One memory I keep close to me with Dad is our Saturday rides to Chimborazo Park and sitting on the hill looking down on the city. He would ask, 'Angie, you coming with Daddy?' He used to tell stories about his brother in the military, and working at one of the warehouses we were looking down on. He always took special time with me. That was a special memory.

"With Mom we used to walk around the yard together and look at her flowers and bushes. She used to say the names of flowers and I would remember the names of the plants. I used to think everything was so beautiful. She used to get on me about breaking off her carnations on her bush and putting it on the side of my hair. She also thought it was funny though. She said, 'I told you about breaking of my flowers!'"

FROM THOMAS AND EVANGELINE'S SONS-IN-LAW (BY MARRIAGE DATE)

First Son-In-Law, Dennis Sr.

"I enjoyed the times and opportunities I had to spend with my father-in-law and mother-in-law. It was a blessing. I saw the way they loved me and cared about me. They took me in the first day. I am very thankful for the time they were here. They showed us how to love each other and how to make the marriage stronger, and how to respect other people. They showed respect to our relationship and children. They taught us how to be mature adults. All the things they taught us during our 39 years of marriage before they passed were transferable because we taught our children how to make it and enjoy on this side of Jordan and what it means to be a family. They even taught and showed us (as men) how to hug and show gratitude for each other. Many days we had the opportunity to see what family means and that's what they displayed.

"Matthew 25:35 (NIV) says, "For I was hungry and you gave me something to eat, I was thirsty and you gave me something to drink, I was a stranger and you invited me in." They got this scripture right. They had Christian principles and taught us about the Bible; we had many conversations. They were what parents should be. In today times, things may have changed, but they gave us a good solid ground and foundation on how we should carry ourselves. I just think about the respect and integrity they gave us. They knew the Lord and the Word and when they kept our children, I knew they were always in a safe place. Our children are grown now, but still remember the love displayed. They treated me as their first son-in-law as their own son. If no one had told me, I would have thought they were my parents. I had parents who raised me well. But my father-in-law and mother-in-law felt like my parents, too.

"Mother-in-law taught me how to cook food I didn't know how to cook, like collard greens. My father-in-law would cook knuckle bones. We learned things during the years just from being around them. They gave us freely their wisdom. They never got into our marriage. If we had marriage disagreements, they would just call to ask if I was okay. They checked on me as if I was their son. Our children and grandchildren got to spend time with them and see the example that they set. They left a legacy seed that is buried in my heart that I will never forget. I can see their smiles. They taught us about going to church and about community and each other.

"They displayed love in every aspect of life. I called her mom and dad over the years because that's how they treated me. We spent so much time together I felt like I was their son."

PRECIOUS MEMORIES

Second Son-In-Law, Virgil

"They were inseparable. Where you saw one, you saw the other. I used to call my father-in-law Pops. I don't know if I was the first to start calling him that. He adopted it and started receiving it. We had some particularly good conversations about life itself. And yes, the Bible, that was normal and a given. Anytime you visited both of them, God was always in the subject and topic either before we left or when we first got to the house.

"Mom was funny. She always called me Son. I used to always tease her about it. I would say, Mom, who's the best son-in-law? You can tell me in my ear. She would say, 'Now you know, Son, I can't tell you that! I love all of you.' I would say, okay, but you can secretly tell me in my ear that I'm the best son-in-law, right?" We both would laugh. I had many great years with her.

"I recall one moment when I had my pickup truck, and I used to haul mulch for her. My mom/mother-in-law would say, 'I got some mulch I need to get. You can go pick it up for me' and I would do that for her. I could sit all day and talk about what good people my father-in-law and mother-in-law were. They never interfered in our marriage unless we asked them too. They would always give advice and say, 'you all love each other.' They used to say that all the time."

Third Son-In-Law, Rickey

"One good memory I have of my mother-in-law, Evangeline, is when she and I would sit around at her house and have some good talks. I also used to love it when she was cooking; oh, so good. The fondest memory I have of my father-in-law, Thomas, is when he and I were sitting on the deck in Charles City and I told him that I wanted to marry his daughter, Verda. He told me that would be the best Father's Day gift that I could give him! We hugged and shook hands. Oh, what a day that was when I asked for permission to marry his daughter."

Fourth Son-In-Law, Chris

"Mother-in-law had a caring heart and showed her love by cooking for us. We often spent the night at their house and would wake up on Saturday morning to a huge breakfast. Even though we were adults with children, we still felt like kids again. She would come into the room on Saturday morning, where we were sleeping, wake us up, and say 'Y'all come on and eat.' It's funny, I remember the sausage, bacon, and corned beef hash. "My father-in-law and I had many talks on the front porch. I learned a lot from Dad and how humble he was."

Last Son-In-Law, Richard

"I really enjoyed talking with my father-in-law as we would sit in a room relaxing, him in the recliner chair and me on the sofa. He always gave me a lot of good advice.

We enjoyed talking about the Lord.

"I remember he would also quote his favorite scripture: Proverbs 3:5-6. I used to love to sit, talk and watch ministries with my mother-in-law on Sundays. We would come over to her house after going to our church in the morning. We would bring her breakfast, I'd make the coffee, and we would eat together while watching a service. She loved watching Charles Stanley Ministries. We would hang around at the house until my father-in-law got home from his church and enjoy him too.

"She was like a second mother to me. She took the place of my mother who had passed when I was 19 years old. She would always say to us, 'Be good to each other.'"

FROM THOMAS AND EVANGELINE'S GRANDCHILDREN (BY AGE)

First Grandchild, Dennis Jr. (DJ)

"His (Grandfather's) humble spirit and smile that he would give me when I would show up in town was an acknowledgement of him being proud of me without a word being spoken. His leg rocking to calm his nerves or to stay awake, I picked (that habit) up. And watching old westerns with him as a kid 'til I fell asleep stands out.

"I remember watching the *Little Shop of Horrors* movie and trying not to act scared because he was in the room with me. He always had the big leather recliner that I would sneak and sit in when he wasn't around to watch TV.

"Her (Grandmother's) special laugh and her warm embrace would always get me. Her favorite thing to say was 'DJ, why do you wait so long to come see your grandma? You know you're not too old for me to pop you!' and then burst out laughing.

"I remember asking her, Am I your favorite grandchild? She would look at me like boy, how you going to ask me that? with a smirk on her face.

"I remember as a child her asking me to play checkers with her and asking me do I want to play 'Gilbert's Way.' I found out later because she didn't have her teeth in, and she was really saying "giveaway" I couldn't stop laughing with her."

Second Grandchild, Shawntrece

"My memories of grandma and granddad; I remember being young and taking that long ride down the country roads of Charles City to visit Grandma and Granddad. I loved visiting during the holidays because I knew this was time I could spend with not only them, but all my cousins. We would eat good, sing, and laugh - and of course - we would get so full we'd find a spot on the floor by Grandad's chair to lay. Those were the best moments.

"Another memory would be just hanging out with Grandma, trying on her church heels, hats, and jewelry. I loved how she would love to rub and play in my hair (whether it was mine or someone else's). She gave the best massages.

"When I brought my son, Vyzhaun, home from the hospital to her home, she had everything set up. I didn't need anything! She had it all. She even helped plan a baby shower for my arrival home. It was perfect. Vyzhaun was her baby! She would always hold him, pray over him, and watch him as he slept; and the baby talk was hilarious. I will forever miss Grandma and Grandpa dearly. My two angels."

Third Grandchild, Dervin

"His (Grandfather's) prayers will always stay within my heart. I can hear him saying, 'oh, come heavenly Father, come now heavenly Dove, with all Thy quickening power, kindle a flame of sacred love.' "I hear my grandmother's precious powerful laugh and smell the sticky white rice and gravy she made for us. "I take to my heart the memories of each of their hands. I remember them. I see them, each and every vein. I feel them on my head and on my heart, always there. His hands were so big and strong, but gentle. I remember putting quarters through his rings without touching the sides of the ring.

"Her hands were small, but full of great strength, she would rub my head as I lay in her lap. She rubbed my head at Aunt Gail's house the day before she went to her heavenly home. That was the last time."

Fourth Grandchild, La'tisha

"We had a quiet relationship. We didn't talk a lot. I just paid attention to how he (Granddaddy) existed. His actions spoke louder than his words. But when he did talk, it was to say something important or nice. Every once in a while, he would throw in a little quiet, funny one liner. You wouldn't see it coming; because you didn't know he was paying attention. But the main thing I remember him saying, was his favorite scripture, 'Trust in the Lord with all your heart and lean not unto your own understanding.' I remember one day, (after he passed), I had been going through a lot personally and I was tired, so very tired of what felt like a long fight. Then it was as if I could hear his voice saying, *'Just trust in the Lord.'* It resonated so much; I posted it on Facebook. September 23, 2020. That was how he lived and what he honestly believed, so that always stood out to me.

"When I was little, my granddaddy would always watch politics, news broadcasts, Westerns, and nature shows. That was the thing that eventually, I came to enjoy - just watching the nature shows with him. We would make random comments about the animals' behaviors or their physical characteristics. Funny enough, I still watch a lot of nature documentaries. I didn't stick with the Westerns so much, but maybe that's where my love for action movies started. I did really enjoy the fast-paced, slick-talking action in the Westerns and now, I really like horses too. I've noticed that now in my thirties I have an appreciation for his love for certain things, different things.

"I used to call him my teddy bear. He had a quiet and calm presence, was always present, and I always got that impression that he really enjoyed having his family around. It didn't matter if it was just one of his kids or all of his kids or the grandkids. If everybody got together, I remember him simply being happy to be there. Seemed as if he just took it all in. It made me feel as though he was dedicated too. Besides Jesus, we were the most important people in the world to him. You just knew that. I miss him every day.

"My grandma (whom I could never say enough about), was my baby, my sweetie, my ace, my pal, my girl. I miss her deeply. I don't know if I can ever truly quantify it the way I feel it. I have a lot of memories of Tweety pretty early on. We always had a special relationship; spending time with her was always a priority for me. Whether it was because Mom (Gail) got in the car to check on her because she had Grandma on her mind. So, we would be in Charles City all of a sudden. Or, if she was not feeling well, we might be up at 2:00 or 3:00 a.m. to go to Charles City. I felt almost immediately that I would do anything for her because I always knew she was special. She was special and precious to me; I never questioned it. I can't remember a time when she wasn't important and dear to me. She treated me like I was gold, and I did everything I could to do the same. She is literally, even at this moment, still a part of me.

"One of my favorite memories was the holiday season. The holiday season was always fantastic! I loved that we used to get together at my grandparents' house. Part of getting ready for that get together was gifts! After Thanksgiving, when she'd finished her shopping, my grandmother would always call me to find out when I would come over to put up Christmas decorations and wrap gifts. It started when I was around thirteen or fourteen years old. She would call and talk to my Mom a little bit, but I always knew the request was coming because then she would ask if I was around or available if I hadn't already jumped into the conversation. She would say, 'you just let me know when you have some time whenever you're available, it's no rush. Let me know when you can come over and help me with the Christmas decorations.' But of course, I'd come over the same week she called. That was my baby, and I was going to help! So, we'd talk about the decorations, she'd ask my opinion on things, and she would let me pick my Christmas gift too. It never took me long to do, but I'd hang out with her and granddaddy for hours after that. And she would always make sure that when I came over, she had cooked something she knew I liked, which was usually pasta, or some type of meat and rice was the go-to for me. She'd make sure I had something to take home and always said, 'Get a container to take some home for Gail and Richard, too!'

"Education was particularly important to both my grandparents. It was something they instilled in the girls and as a result, it was instilled in me as well. I knew all the things people said about why it was important and sure, I agreed. But my silent motivation was my grandparents and my mom. It was them I carried in my heart. I think about both my graduation days and how terrible the weather was. When I got my bachelor's, it was terribly hot and humid, and graduation was outside! When I got my master's, it was freezing cold. And still, both times, despite how hard the temperatures must've been on them and the crowded, long-distance walks challenging their mobility, they were right there. They never complained. There was a smile on their face every single time, the entire time. Tweety was beaming, truly. In fact, she was so excited, she took my master's graduation cap and put it on! That made my heart so full. I told her to keep it, she'd earned it just as much as me. One of my favorite moments, and pictures, to this day."

Fifth Grandchild, Rickey Jr.

"My granddad was a stoic man who had seen decades of seasons. When my grandad talked, you listened. Not just with your ears but also with your spirit, absorbing the wisdom that seeped from his strong voice. We sat, two generations entwined, looking out to the street watching airplanes skim by our heads and shaking the house at times.

"Cutting the grass early in the morning to get the body flowing with pure energy. I would cut the yard, and my legs would feel strong with accomplishment. This green thumb memory isn't just about the lawn, it's about the bond between my grandad – who shaped my life - and I.

"Grandma's exclusive spaghetti. Think about a warm kitchen, laughter from all the first-floor rooms on Ingleside Drive and a countertop packed with southern goods. Gracefully walking, my grandma randomly checking the spaghetti, her hands moved with grace, the same hands that cradled me as a child. I plated the spaghetti, took that first bite, an orchestra of flavors and love. It was not just a meal; it was a legacy. After that first plate was finished, she would catch me going for seconds and never forgot to tell me, 'Grandma knows what you like,'" smiling from cheek-to-cheek, I gave her praise as if she needed it. It came to the point over the years that this particular dish was exclusively made for me."

Sixth Grandchild, Jemiah

"One of my favorite memories about my grandparents is how the family used to gather on Sundays in their home and fellowship with food, love, and laughter. The holidays were ten times the thrill. Grandma and Grandpa were always ready for our big family to visit. I remember, even at my adult age, sitting in my grandma's lap or sitting by my grandpa's feet listening to them laugh and tell stories. Their presence was so peaceful that sometimes no words were spoken, just love being felt."

Seventh and Eighth Grandchildren (respectively),

"They always gave us snacks. We couldn't wait to go into the pantry where all the snacks were and sit at the kitchen table watching cartoons. Grandad would say, 'Y'all eat!' or 'Help yourself.' We remember how we used to watch the black and white movies with Grandad."

FROM THOMAS AND EVANGELINE'S SURVIVING SIBLINGS

Thomas' Baby Sister, Rev. Janice

"Thomas was my first Bible study teacher after I accepted the Lord Jesus Christ as my Savior. I had relocated to Virginia and was living with him and his family at the time. Our parents had taught me about the Lord Jesus, but after I came to know Him for myself, I had so many questions. And as God ordained it, Thomas was accessible to me, and he answered each of them with love and patience. While living with my brother, I joined the church he attended which was across town from my new residence. So, one Sunday, I decided to visit a church that was closer to home. During the invitation to discipleship, the pastor said, 'If you do not know that you would go to heaven if you died right now, you need to come!' I did not go up but, as a new Christian, I started to doubt my salvation. I did not know if I would go to heaven if I died right then because I did not feel saved. I could not wait to get home and call my brother, Thomas. When I told him my dilemma, Thomas recited John 3:16 calmly and deliberately and asked if I believed it. I said that I did. Then he said, 'The Word of God does not say, 'whosoever feels like it' shall be saved, but 'whosoever believes in Him' shall be saved.' That settled it for me! The doubt left! And the next Sunday, I drove across town to my home church.

"Evangeline was wise and discerning. In the natural, I would say that she was a counselor in her own right. But in the spiritual, she was operating in several gifts of the Holy Spirit, namely, the word of wisdom, the word of knowledge, and the discernment of spirits. Evangeline was direct and to the point. She did not beat around the bush, so to speak. If she saw, discerned, or heard that I was dealing with something, she addressed it. Sometimes, I did not feel like addressing it, but she had a way of getting me to open up. I experienced Evangeline as firm, loving, honest, and encouraging. I tended to leave the presence of her company better off than when I came."

Thomas' Baby Brother, Pastor Russell

"Thomas and Evangeline have always been dear to me because they loved the Lord. I remember when I graduated from high school. I came to Charles City, and I stayed with one of my brothers in Virginia. We all worked at the same place, Crawford Manufactory. I made up my mind that I would go back home, but I wasn't saved at that time. I was 18 years old, and he (Thomas) came to me while I was on the job and told me he hated to see me go. But in a way he was glad I was going back home because if I stayed, I would turn into an alcoholic. It was heavy, but it helped me. And he always talked to me about being saved and giving my life to Jesus. He planted that seed in me and today I can say I am saved, and I don't drink and haven't in over 40 years.

"The last time Thomas came to our Fourth of July celebration, one of his children said they would stay with Evangeline, because she was sick, so he could go to North Carolina. We were outside talking; he had been going through his own sickness prior to coming. While we were outside talking, a storm was coming and I told Thomas to go into the house because it was about to pour down, but he didn't go into the house. After everything settled down we started back talking and I asked him why he didn't go into the house during the storm. He said he was having a good time holding the tent. That was an example of having a good time even though you are going through a storm–.

"(Once) I was in Richmond because we were having a family gathering, having a good time and all of a sudden my son started crying. He had stings everywhere and we took him to the emergency room, and they gave him something, but it didn't work. We went back to Thomas and Evangeline's home. And she did an old remedy. She took vinegar and pennies and rubbed his body all over, and within a few minutes the stings were gone.

"Evangeline was working at Crawford, and I was there too. She didn't like to be called by her nickname, Little Jack at work. She and her co-workers were walking, and I called out, "Little Jack, Little Jack!" She wouldn't look back. I told Thomas that I called her Little Jack, and she acted like she didn't know who I was. She said, 'I didn't know who you were calling me Little Jack.' Even after then when I would call her Little Jack, and she would ignore me."

Thomas' Sister, Joyce

"Thomas reminded me so much of our daddy. He was my older brother, and I didn't know how to talk to him. I really didn't see him because he had moved to Richmond, and I left home at an early age. It was like being with my dad again after Dad had passed. I really loved my brother's hugs; they made me feel special. I knew that he loved me just by the way of his quiet presence. Though I didn't see him that much, when we saw each other, it was like we were picking things up from where we left off.

"Evangeline made me feel special. She knew how to pull conversation out of me. I am not a big talker, but she knew how to get me to talk about what was going on with me. She was a fun person who always had something good happening when she came around."

Evangeline's Baby Sister, Betty (better known as Bay)

"We had happy times with my sister, Evangeline and our brother-in-law, Thomas. I remember when we moved to

Richmond, Evangeline called and said can we come and stay with you in Richmond. It was a blessing because I was lonely and missed them too. They were my heart, I loved them, and they loved me. We went through good times and bad times together. We cried together and laughed together. We always had a good time together.

"We used to have holidays together when we were younger. My sister and I used to sew and make our own things. We would come home after school and church and create things. We always enjoyed each other. We did everything together. Our mom would set us down and ask, who wants to do this or that chore? We would say which one we want to do. We had a close relationship. We would have fun, and our dad and mom would give us rewards for doing things.

"I came over to their daughter, Gail's house after Thomas had passed. And I was talking to Evangeline. I said, 'Sis, can I ask you something?' She said, 'Sure.' I asked, 'Do you have any kind of regrets about anything?' She said, 'No. I've been happy all my life, with my children, husband, mom, and I love you all and I wouldn't take anything for it.' She gave me a smile and hugged me. I said, 'Sis you going to be all right because God is going to take care of you. And we are going to be here for you.' Evangeline said, 'I'm not worrying. I talked to God and me and him are going to be together. I'm going home and I'm going to be with him. I'm going to heaven.' She smiled. We used to do that when we were young. We would ask each other, 'Why are you sitting there? What are you thinking about? Is there anything you feel you have regret for?' And then we would start talking. I know Thomas and Evangeline loved each other. Nobody could take that away. They were my heart. I miss them."

FROM THOMAS AND EVANGELINE'S BEST FRIENDS

Deacon and Deaconess Gilbert, Sr., and Edith H.

"They were God-fearing people. We knew them for many, many years before they passed away to be with the Lord. We received Thomas and Evangeline's family into our family of two sons. Thomas and Evangeline asked me and my wife, Edith, to be godparents to their baby daughter, Angeline and the other daughters asked if we could be their godparents too. We said yes we would. This was a great blessing to us. During this time, Thomas and I were ordained as deacons and Evangeline and my wife, as deaconesses. We were members of the same church where we worshiped and praised God together.

We traveled and had a lot of fun attending many family functions together! We were the best of friends. We miss them so much. Thank God for so many blessings."

PRECIOUS MEMORIES

Deacon and Deaconess Willie Sr. and Clara B.

Evangeline had a green thumb. I got my first flower plants from her. She had healthy plants inside of a closet. I still have those plants, which beautify my home today.

When Evangeline and her family moved to Charles City, Virginia, I would tease her that they lived such a distance away that we had to stop for a lunch break before arriving to her home for a visit. I called her my baby.

Deacon Roberson was a devoted Christian gentleman. A devoted husband and father of his five daughters. We really miss them."

More Precious Memories: Precious <u>Envelopes of Family Letters</u> Written, Gifts, and Family Routines

Letters are a great way to keep memories of people and special moments in your life alive. Thomas and Evangeline treasured the letters given to them from loved ones and friends. Thomas gave his daughter, Gail, an envelope filled with letters written to him, Evangeline, and from family members, one Sunday evening in June 2018. He told his daughter he wanted her to take it because he knew she could do something valuable with it.

She said, "If you'd like, I can put them in a nice picture album and label the letters and give it back to you." He said, "No. I want you to have it. I know you will think of something to do with them since you are a writer." She told him, "I don't know what to do with it!" He only replied, "You will." He smiled; and she took the letters and told him thank you."

"Sadly, just a little than year later, Gail would be confronted with their sudden passing and many memories through the letters. The letters she didn't know what to do with now have a clearer purpose in this book. She could reflect on the letters and have authentic dates and times of various events in the book.

The letters reflected the loving relationship between Thomas and his mother, and Evangeline and her mother, as well as other family members. In their beautiful penmanship. Evangeline's letters from her mother would let her know how the family was doing and ask her to visit soon. She would always end her letters with 'Love Annie V.' or 'Love Mom.' Thomas' letters from his mother would always say how glad she was to hear from him and that his father sent his love. She spoke often of how much she missed him and the family. She shared what she was doing at home: working at pulling plants, putting in and grounding tobacco. When she was done writing, she frequently closed the letters 'Take care now and pray. May God bless us and keep us safe from harm until we meet again.' Or 'Take care, kiss the children for me. Hope to see you soon. Give my love to Evangeline and the children.' There were letters also from Thomas' brother in the military. He used to come and spend time with Thomas and the family.

Letters and More to Beloved Family Members

Letters from Evangeline were given to the children through the oldest daughter, Mary, after their deaths. It was an emotional moment for all of the girls. Evangeline wrote these letters to each child over a decade ago. What treasure to behold.

Gifts

Thomas and Evangeline gave their children gifts and encouragement to show how proud they were of them during times of achievements, but also "just because" and "thinking of you" gifts to say they loved them. They were always generous. This is a behavior passed on from generation to generation. Thomas and Evangeline girls recall that there were times when visiting the home of both sets of grandparents, they would give them something nice before they left their houses. It could be money, candy, or presents. If it was something small enough, their grandparents would take their hand, place the gift or money inside, then fold their fingers over it and gently pat it. They'd say thank you and give them a good squeeze each time.

Saturday Family Routines and Responsibilities

To keep the home of the Roberson family with seven running well, there were routines in the house that happened every week, month, and/or year. Evangeline kept the house spotless and taught the children to clean regularly to keep germs from collecting;, and by dusting the way she learned growing up (due to her mother's illnesses). She carried this household routine with her into the marriage. In the spring and summer there was thorough cleaning from the floors to the walls, furniture, and windows.

Sundays were always busy with church ministry. It was usually an all-day affair so their mom, Evangeline, and some of the children, mainly the oldest ones, Mary and Linda, would cook Sunday's meal on Saturday. Cooking on Saturday instead of Sunday was also due to their parents not wanting the children to do anything related to work on Sunday including cooking, ironing, or washing clothes. Sunday was holy and a rest from everyday activities. They also prepared their Sunday attire on Saturday. School homework was also finished prior to Sunday. These chores had to be done prior to going out for the day on Saturday with friends. It also ensured when the family got home on Sunday, they only needed to warm the food. This was also done in case they had to go back to church later that day for another event. This routine turned out to be a helpful one. There were seven family members, so they didn't go out to dinner a lot. They did have some amazing meals, and the children learned how to cook well.

Other Routines

Wednesday night's routine was the regular Bible study held at home, if we weren't able to go to church on

Wednesday night due to my mother not feeling well. Each person would take turns reading the scripture and even singing and praying together. We had family fun routines too. We regularly went on trips, family reunions, and had holiday gatherings. Family get-togethers remained the heartbeat of this close-knit family. The family always had a lot of fun with one another, playing games, watching shows together, laughing and talking and the girls being the best of friends, even now.

> *These commandments that I give you today are to be on your hearts Impress them on your children. Talk about them when you sit at home and when you walk along the road, when you lie down and when you get up.*
>
> **Deuteronomy 6:6-7 (NIV)**

I DO! THE LOVE STORY

"A HOUSEHOLD TRADITION"

Friday Night
It's Friday night and time
to setup the living room
with chairs and colorful blankets on the floor

It looked like a child's play area
A night for movies or playing games
Which one will it be?

Who would take home the winning prize
as they study, one another in a game
to see what each would choose

Laughing, eating and hanging out with loved ones
skillfully playing in a game of fun
yet competitive and hoping the other team will lose

A lifelong countless family tradition,
one can measure
something they will remember and always treasure

9/14/17
By Gail Wright

"THE FAMILY TRADITION: HOLIDAY HOMETOWN COUNTDOWN"

The aroma of glazed ham and turkey spread,
gravy passed by my sensitive nose
it made me hungry and thrilled about the season

As my family moved about in the house
with anticipation and festive clothes
a celebrated holiday feeling, Thanksgiving
and Christmas being the reason

Interior decoration hanging all around
mainly on the inside of the house and
front harden beige door

Ornaments pulled from the attic
that my dad brought down
cheerfully preparing food, for families of six or more

Smiling as they enter the home
coming to share their recipes and love

As they are greeted with shalom
being remembered as Prince of Peace, Christ from above

Family dinner tradition being passed down
to the next generation for a holiday countdown
gathering hometown

9/4/17
By Gail Wright

CHAPTER 4
The Secret Sauce to Thomas and Evangeline's Long Marriage

What is a successful marriage? What would you tell your younger self about being married for an extended period of time? It is said that marriage is a marathon, not a sprint. Thomas and Evangeline were two people with dissimilar personalities joining together in love and holy matrimony from different family backgrounds and views. However, they came together to build their marriage in the way they felt it should be. There are some specific pillars of a successful, healthy, and lasting marriage relationship. Thomas and Evangeline's children and family witnessed them demonstrating these to sustain their marriage over the decades. The most important contributor that they talked about was prayer. They believed in praying together about life's situations and allowing the Holy Spirit to lead them in what to do. They decided that keeping Jesus in the center of the marriage was crucial and not optional. They also prayed with their children when situations arose and encouraged their children to do the same in their marriages and families.

Thomas and Evangeline taught their family to never stop praying, believe God for the answer, and not to get into a rush to do things their own way, but instead trust God. They told their children that life was not perfect nor was marriage, but what each person put into the relationship is important as partners. They taught them to let God lead their marriage relationship and family. Thomas and Evangeline understood that even with these pillars there is no perfect marriage or person but a perfect God to help in a relationship.

Marriage Pillars

- Prayer,
- Communication,
- Compromise,
- Commitment,
- Validation,
- Acceptance,
- Trust,
- Compassion,
- Intimacy,

THE SECRET SAUCE

- Appreciation,
- Partnership,
- Consideration,
- Intentionality,
- Positivity,
- Empathy,
- Mutual Respect,
- Affection,
- Love,
- Honesty

Hey, Did You Know?
Marriage and Divorce Data for the U.S.

Number of marriages: 2,065,905
Marriage rate: 6.2 per 1,000 total population
Number of divorces: 673,989
(45 reporting states and D.C.)
Divorce rate: 2.4 per 1,000 population
(45 reporting states and D.C.)

S*ources: National Marriage and Divorce Rate Trends for 2000-2022*

https://www.cdc.gov/nchs/fastats/marriage-divorce.htm

I DO! THE LOVE STORY

PICTURES FROM 50ᵀᴴ ANNIVERSARY CELEBRATION

Thomas 69 years old and Evangeline 67 years old

*Thomas and Evangeline
kissing after cutting wedding cake*

"HE & SHE"

(This poem was written for and read to Thomas and Evangeline on their 50th Anniversary)

She Is:
Beautiful,
Artistic
Always encouraging a saddened heart
Beyond helpful, doing more than her part

She Is:
Funny, full of life and surprises
Seeing her is like watching the early morning sun rise

He Is:
Strong,
Dependable
Among men he stands as a pillar
The perfect example of a Godly man's figure

He Is:
Calm, laid back, peaceable in spirit.
When he speaks, there's purpose.
And you can hear it.

They Are:
Genuine,
Understanding,
Supportive
So wonderful to talk with

They Are
A Vision of life
A Vision of love
A vision of what God above designed a marriage to be.
A love beyond infinity
Perfected in eternity.

They Made Us
Strong,
Times the world did not have a good
relationship with our plans.
In prayer, they made a stand.

They Made Us:
Wise,
in Godly wisdom they gave advice.

Together We Are:
Here,
because of their sacrifice

Together We Are:
Here,
because of he and she
Their love stands 50 years strong and will ever be.
The example of God's love shining brightly

11/2010

By La'tisha Roberson (granddaughter)
Dedicated on behalf of your proud grandchildren

THE SECRET SAUCE

Fifty-Ninth Wedding Anniversary Breakdown

Decades: 5.9

◇◇◇◇◇◇◇◇◇

Years: 59

◇◇◇◇◇◇◇◇◇

Months: 70

◇◇◇◇◇◇◇◇◇

Weeks: 3078

◇◇◇◇◇◇◇◇◇

Days: 21,549

◇◇◇◇◇◇◇◇◇

Hours: 517,183

◇◇◇◇◇◇◇◇◇

Minutes: 31,031,003

◇◇◇◇◇◇◇◇◇

Seconds: 1,861,860,168

◇◇◇◇◇◇◇◇◇

CHAPTER 5
LIFE HAPPENINGS: ADVANCED YEARS

Ready, really? Thomas and Evangeline advanced in life. They got older and dealt with illnesses in their own body. They matured even more in their marriage and supported one another and took care of each other in their maturing ages. They would always be heard saying, "You all love and take care of one another." Those hearing it would reply affirmatively. They continued to serve God, family, others, and each other until the end.

It is not known when the unexpected will happen, but when it does, there needs to be a safe place to go to deal with the trauma; like going to God, family, church, and friends. Don't deal with it alone because everyone faces heartache and pain. It is how it is responded to that will make the difference. Sometimes one may feel they know how they would respond, but they find out they don't truly know until the time comes.

The year 2019 was the children's time to discover . At the end of the year, traumatic events stunned the family. Tuesday morning of Thanksgiving week, the family received a call informing them that Thomas was taken to the hospital after suffering a heart attack. The family, praying for a full recovery, took turns rotating in and out of the hospital, with Mary being on-site and on call for any medical concerns. On Thanksgiving Day nearly everyone stopped by to see him, assuring he wouldn't be alone. It was the first holiday they wouldn't be all together in decades. After Thanksgiving, he had triple heart bypass surgery. And thankfully, he was on his way to recovery. Over the next couple of weeks, there was this procedure and that procedure. And this recommendation and others. It seemed like he'd do better, then something would get a little hairy; right up until December 14 when suddenly, late in the evening, he took a turn for the worse. Many intercessory prayers were released for his recovery. Yet, hours later, he passed after having multiple complications. This was a gut-wrenching loss. Thomas had never spent time admitted to the hospital. That had been Evangeline. But Thomas did his doctor's appointments, took his required medications, and that was it. To have him admitted to the hospital and never come out; it broke everyone's hearts.

Over the next week, the heaviness of grief trailed funeral planning. The girls did what they had always done, they got together and did what was needed as a family with help from loved ones, friends, and church members who checked in and offered support through prayers, calls, visits, and love gifts and meals.

Evangeline was quiet. Often listening attentively to planning and making decisions where she felt was needed. Finally, it was time to lay Thomas to rest. December 19 arrived with a heaviness befitting the loss of a great family man. But grief wasn't done with us yet. Before we could lay Thomas to rest, five days after he passed, about an hour before his funeral, Evangeline died.

This was truly "until death do us part." They genuinely loved each other and did everything together including departing this side of Earth within days of each other. The family trusted that Thomas and Evangeline met each other on the other side in heaven shortly afterwards because they were ready to go home to be with the Lord. And so began a year of uncertainty. A year of birthdays, holidays, random Sundays, and a global pandemic that would separate families and loved ones for our safety.

At a time when our family desperately needed to be together, they had to find ways to be together across distance, space, and time. For almost a year, they grieved until the holiday season came around again and what had been a joyous time for them all became one that was uncertain and heavy with memories. The family stumbled through Thanksgiving and creeped toward the one-year anniversary of Thomas' passing knowing that the one-year anniversary of Evangeline's passing was only five days away.

But before they could make it there, tragedy struck again. Mary, the firstborn child, who had so diligently managed each after-death responsibility, had a sudden health crisis. She was struck with what we would later learn was a brain stroke and passed away in December 2020. Three significant losses, all during the holidays and back-to-back in December. Our hearts were shattered for a third time. The horrific pain experienced during each of the family losses has been turned into gain. And the heartaches, tears, and sorrows have been blossoming into a message (this book) to assist and encourage those married both new, long-term, and other varying stages to serve the Almighty God with all their heart until the end.

While writing this book in 2024, it has been five years since the passing of both Thomas and Evangeline. Walking through the storm of their deaths and respecting the process of grief was not easy, but God carried the family through it. Healing gradually and gracefully came to each child and family member, but differently. Some walked through in a short period of grief, and some took longer as they rested in God's love and trusted Him to bring them through. They held on to Jesus, their Hope, Counselor, Healer, and Comforter when they had to question things they didn't understand. They chose to trust God and His faithfulness to carry them through every situation. It was a real, "until death do us part" experience. We are all grateful for the time we were blessed to share with our parents, mighty man, and woman of God, and we look forward to the heavenly reunion. Death (on Earth) is a gateway to heaven (life). And heaven, as we read in Hebrews 13:14 (KJV) is an eternal city. "For here we have no continuing city, but we seek the one to come."

It Is Not Goodbye but See You Later on The Other Side - HEAVEN!

In romance stories everyone loves a happy ending. Thomas' and Evangeline's love story had the happiest ending. They loved the Lord, themselves, and others. They served God until the end of their lives. They loved their family and friends. They told their family that they were ready to go home and see Jesus. Thomas and Evangeline would encourage everyone they met to allow God to use them and be effective for God. When we come to the end of our lives, we want to be able to recite the words found in Second Timothy.

> *I have fought a good fight, I have finished my course, I have kept the faith: Henceforth there is laid up for me a crown of righteousness, which the Lord, the righteous judge, shall give me at that day: and not to me only, but unto all them also that love his appearing.*
>
> **2 Timothy 4:7-8 (KJV)**

POEMS FROM THE OBITUARIES

"Heaven Bound"

In Memory of Deacon Thomas Roberson

He was heaven bound to live with Jesus,
a time without end.
Everyday walked with Jesus through his
journey from the beginning to the end

Always encouraged one to trust and obey.
Very willing to take life's situations day-by-day
Endless love for Jesus his Savior and friend
Nothing could separate him from his love
for God, thick or thin.

Being encouraged to know that heaven, the kingdom, is
for every saved human.
Our life, for it, God has a divine plan.
Up and running the Christian race
Never giving up, but keeping the faith and pace
Diligently seeking God, running your own race,
and then he will see you one glorious day face-to-face

12/19/19

By Gail Wright, daughter

LIFE HAPPENINGS: ADVANCED YEARS

"GOING UP YONDER"

In Memory of Deaconess Evangeline Roberson

Gone up yonder to be with my
Lord is the message she sends.
Onward Christian soldier, walked with Jesus through her
journey from the beginning to the end.
In her actions, emulated a Proverbs 31 woman to her
husband, children, and kin as God's servant and as His
friend.
Nothing separated her from the love of God,
as she trusts and obey.
God is good, she would say.

Unapologetically, committed to Godly living.
Purposefully loving and serving people by caring,
praying, encouraging, and giving

Yes! She said to God while running the Christian race.
Option to give up? Never! But instead
kept the faith and pace.

Now she has had a dream of strutting with no cane. Even
practiced for a couple of weeks, enjoying the confidence
and victory she would gain.

Days later we now know, it was her healing she saw. She
is walking around heaven, free with no pain.
Even until the end of her journey,
she would be of one accord.

Ready and heaven bound, "Gone Up Yonder" to be with her husband, and Jesus Christ, her Lord.
12/27/19

By Gail Wright, daughter

His lord said to him, 'Well done, **good and faithful servant***; you were* **faithful** *over a few things, I will make you ruler over many things. Enter into the joy of your lord.'*

- Matthew 25:21 (NKJV)

LIFE HAPPENINGS: ADVANCED YEARS

LEAVING A FAMILY AND SPIRITUAL LEGACY

Don't waste your time! Thomas and Evangeline left a spiritual legacy. It was a family spiritual legacy that we all can observe. God showed up in their lives. They made their lives count on purpose. No Regrets! Thomas and Evangeline would ask, "what is the spiritual legacy you want to leave to share with others to grow closer to Jesus?"

These are some of the things they taught at the end of their lives on Earth Family - pray, obey, and trust in God
Children learn the Word
Live out the Word
Grow in the Word - it brings life
Have faith in the Word of God.
Love God, self, and others
Serve God in church and ministry
Be about God's business
Achieve God's Purpose for your life
Be Saved! Surrender you lives to Christ

> *So then, be careful how you walk, not as unwise people but as wise, 16 making the most of your time, because the days are evil. 17 Therefore do not be foolish but understand what the will of the Lord is.*
> **Ephesians 5: 15-17**
> **(New American Standard Bible, NASB)**

CHAPTER 6
Uplifting Marriage Resources

A BLESSED MAN:
What Does a Good Husband Look Like?

Ephesians 5:28-31 (NASB) - So, husbands also ought to love their own wives as their own bodies. He who loves his own wife loves himself; or no one ever hated his own flesh, but nourishes and cherishes it, just as Christ also does the church, because we are parts of His body. For this reason a man shall leave his father and his mother and be joined to his wife, and the two shall become one flesh.

A BLESSED WOMAN:
What Does a Good Wife Look Like?

Proverbs 31:10-31 (NASB) - An excellent wife, who can find her? For her worth is far above jewels. The heart of her husband trusts in her, and he will have no lack of gain. She does him good and not evil All the days of her life....

James 1:17- (AMP) - Every good thing given and every perfect gift is from above; it comes down from the Father of lights [the Creator and Sustainer of the heavens], in whom there is no variation [no rising or setting] or shadow [a]cast by His turning for He is perfect and never changes.

LOVE AND MARRIAGE VERSES FOR COUPLES

Proverbs 18:22 (AMP) "He who finds a wife finds a [true and faithful] good thing and obtains favor from the Lord."

Ephesians 5:32-33 (NKJV) This is a great mystery, but I speak concerning Christ and the church. [33] Nevertheless let each one of you in particular so love his own wife as himself, and let the wife see that she respects her husband.

Genesis 2:24(NIV) "That is why a man leaves his father and mother and is united to his wife, and they become one flesh."

Ephesians 5:25 (NIV) "Husbands, love your wives, just as Christ loved the church and gave himself up for her."

Titus 2:4 (AMPC) So that they will wisely train the young women to be sane and sober of mind (temperate, disciplined) and to love their husbands and their children.

1 John 4:12 (NIV) "No one has ever seen God; but if we

love one another, God lives in us, and his love is made complete in us."

1 Corinthians 13:4 (NIV) "Love is patient, love is kind. It does not envy, it does not boast, it is not proud.

Matthew 19:6 (NIV) So they are no longer two, but one flesh. Therefore, what God has joined together, let no one separate."

1 Corinthians 16:14 (NIV) Do everything in love.

1 Peter 4:8 (NIV) Above all, love each other deeply, because love covers a multitude of sins.

1 John 4:7 (NIV) Dear friends, let us love one another, for love comes from God. Everyone who loves has been born of God and knows God.

Proverbs 3:3 (NIV) Let love and faithfulness never leave you; bind them around your neck, write them on the tablet of your heart.

Ephesians 4:2-3 (NASB) with all humility and gentleness, with patience, bearing with one another in love, being diligent to keep the unity of the Spirit in the bond of peace.

Lamentations 5:19 (AMP) But You, O Lord, reign forever; Your throne endures from generation to [all] generation.

Hebrews 11:1-2 (The Message Bible, MSG) The fundamental fact of existence is that this trust in God, is the firm foundation under everything that makes life worth living. It's our handle on what we can't see. The act of faith is what distinguished our ancestors, set them above the crowd.

Romans 12:9-9 (NIV) Love must be sincere. Hate what is evil; cling to what is good.

Psalms 18:1-2 (NKJV) I will love You, O Lord, my strength. The Lord is my rock and my fortress and my deliverer; My God, my strength, in whom I will trust; My shield and the horn of my salvation, my stronghold.

Matthew 5:13 (NKJV) Believers Are Salt and Light. You are the salt of the earth; but if the salt loses its flavor, how shall it be seasoned? It is then good for nothing but to be thrown out and trampled underfoot by men.

Joshua 24:15 (AMP) ...but as for me and my house, we will serve the Lord.

Hebrews 12:2 (NIV) Fixing our eyes on Jesus, the pioneer and perfecter of faith. For the joy set before him he endured the cross, scorning its shame, and sat down at the right hand of the throne of God.

GRATITUDE FOR HIS FAITHFULNESS
(NIV scriptures listed)

Psalm 108: 3-4 - I will praise you, Lord, among the nations; I will sing of you among the peoples. For great is your love, higher than the heavens; your faithfulness reaches to the skies.

UPLIFTING MARRIAGE RESOURCES

Psalm 106:1 - Praise the Lord. Give thanks to the Lord, for he is good; his love endures forever.

Romans 15:13 - May the God of hope fill you with all joy and peace as you trust in him, so that you may overflow with hope by the power of the Holy Spirit.

Psalm 21:6 - Surely you have granted him unending blessings and made him glad with the joy of your presence.

Philippians 4:19 - And my God will meet all your needs according to the riches of his glory in Christ Jesus.

Jeremiah 29:11 – "For I know the plans I have for you," declares the Lord, "plans to prosper you and not to harm you, plans to give you hope and a future.

1 Corinthians 15:57 - But thanks be to God! He gives us the victory through our Lord Jesus Christ.

Psalm 37:23-24 - The Lord makes firm the steps of the one who delights in him; though he may stumble, he will not fall, for the Lord upholds him with his hand.

Hebrews 13:20-21 - Now may the God of peace, who through the blood of the eternal covenant brought back from the dead our Lord Jesus, that great Shepherd of the sheep, equip you with everything good for doing his will, and may he work in us what is pleasing to him, through Jesus Christ, to whom be glory for ever and ever. Amen.

Psalm 119:105 - Your word is a lamp for my feet, a light on my path.

2 Corinthians 2:14 - But thanks be to God, who always leads us as captives in Christ's triumphal procession and uses us to spread the aroma of the knowledge of him everywhere.

Colossians 3:16 - Let the message of Christ dwell among you richly as you teach and admonish one another with all wisdom through psalms, hymns, and songs from the Spirit, singing to God with gratitude in your hearts.

Hebrews 12:2 - Fixing our eyes on Jesus, the pioneer and perfecter of faith. For the joy set before him he endured the cross, scorning its shame, and sat down at the right hand of the throne of God.

Matthew 5:16 - In the same way, let your light shine before others, that they may see your good deeds and glorify your Father in heaven.

BLESSINGS OVER THE FAMILY

Deuteronomy 28:1-6 (NKJV) - Now it shall come to pass, if you diligently obey the voice of the Lord your God, to observe carefully all His commandments which I command you today, that the Lord your God will set you high above all nations of the earth. And all these blessings shall come upon you and overtake you, because you obey the voice of the Lord your God: "Blessed shall you be in the city, and blessed shall you be in the country. "Blessed shall be the fruit of your body, the produce of your ground and the increase of your herds, the increase of your cattle and the offspring of your flocks. "Blessed shall be your basket and your kneading bowl. "Blessed shall you be when you come in, and blessed shall you be when you go out."

Deuteronomy 28:8 (KJV) - The Lord shall command the blessing upon thee in thy storehouses, and in all that thou settest thine hand unto; and he shall bless thee in the land which the Lord thy God giveth thee.

Hebrews 6:14 (KJV) - Saying, Surely blessing I will bless thee, and multiplying I will multiply thee.

Numbers 6:25-26 (NKJV) - The Lord make His face shine upon you and be gracious to you; The Lord lift up His countenance upon you and give you peace.

PRAYER OF SALVATION

But what does it say? "The word is near you, in your mouth and in your heart" (that is, the word of faith which we preach): **that if you confess with your mouth the Lord Jesus and believe in your heart that God has raised Him from the dead, you will be saved.** *For with the heart one believes unto righteousness, and with the mouth confession is made unto salvation.*

Romans 10:8-10 (NKJV)

REPEAT THIS PRAYER:

Father, I ask You to forgive me for my sins. I confess that You are Lord, and I ask You to come into my heart and be Lord and Savior over my life. I believe Jesus died for my sins and You raised Him from the dead with all power in His hand and I thank You that I am saved. Amen

If you said this prayer, Welcome to the family of God.

ENCOURAGING QUOTES

Marriage

"Let the wife make the husband glad to come home and let him make her sorry to see him leave." Martin Luther
"A word of encouragement from a teacher to a child can change a life. A word of encouragement from a spouse can save a marriage. A word of encouragement from a leader can inspire a person to reach her potential."

John C. Maxwell

Life

"Life's most persistent and urgent question is, What are you doing for others?"
Martin Luther King, Jr.

"Life is ten percent what happens to you and ninety percent how you respond to it."
Lou Holtz

Love

"Spread love everywhere you go. Let no one ever come to you without leaving happier. "
Mother Teresa

"You can give without loving, but you can never love without giving."
Robert Louis Stevenson

Grief

"…Faith is incredibly important because you will become overwhelmed with what's happening and you will have waves of grief, but when you turn to your faith, I believe God will give you waves of grace to get through it."
Joel Osteen

All quotes from www.brainyquote.com

I DO! THE LOVE STORY

WORD SEARCH: ATTRIBUTES OF LOVE & MARRIAGE 1

Find the words in the puzzle

```
E  G  F  O  R  G  I  V  E  N  E  S  S
F  N  S  P  E  L  H  E  A  L  T  H  C
C  A  G  U  A  V  C  D  F  A  I  T  H
F  K  M  A  S  R  O  A  F  T  I  P  T
R  U  D  I  G  E  T  L  R  Z  H  R  H
T  G  N  S  L  E  J  N  Y  E  O  A  G
R  U  E  P  E  Y  Z  N  E  X  P  Y  I
U  A  S  A  L  T  I  M  E  R  E  E  N
S  L  Q  R  E  S  P  E  C  T  S  R  E
T  I  T  Y  A  Y  T  I  N  U  E  E  T
E  F  T  N  E  M  T  I  M  M  O  C  A
F  E  H  B  I  B  L  E  T  G  K  L  D
R  E  C  R  E  A  T  I  O  N  A  L  Z
X  B  E  P  R  E  S  E  N  T  C  P  S
E  M  P  A  T  H  Y  T  L  I  G  H  T
```

Unity Bible Fun Care Trust Be Present Family
Time Respect Prayer Life Salt Engage Hope
Partners Date-Night Commitment Light
Forgiveness Empathy Recreation Health Faith

UPLIFTING MARRIAGE RESOURCES

WORD SEARCH: ATTRIBUTES OF LOVE & MARRIAGE 2

Find the words in the puzzle.

```
N O I T A C I N U M M O C
P I S B E L J O S E G E C
C I H U I V C G O D H N P
H K H S S I O T F S I C A
R Y D S E E S L R W Y O T
Y G R S N O J V Y O A U I
R H O M E O Z N M V C R E
E A S A L J I P E S Z A N
T S U P P O R T I N G G C
N H T M A R R I A G E E E
E F I N A N C E B L A G D
C A F F E C T I O N E L D
F N H C R U H C R S O R Z
```

Love   Vows   Relationship   God   Supporting
Home   Patience   Jesus   Communication   Encourage
Church   Marriage   Finance   Center   Affection

123

Bibliography

1. AmericanGreetings.com, Anniversary Gift Guide - 59th Anniversary- Traditional 59th Anniversary Gift Ideas: Philanthropy-Modern 59th Anniversary Gift Ideas: Marble, American Greetings, https://www.americangreetings.com/inspiration/wedding-anniversary-gift-guide/59th-year, accessed September 28, 2024

2. Bibilica.com. (1978,1983,2011). *New International Version-Holy Bible.* Gateway, Retrieved September 25, 2024, from http://gateway.com
https://www.biblegateway.com/passage/?search=mark%2010%3A6-9&version=NIV; accessed September 25, 2024
https://www.biblegateway.com/passage/?search=Psalms%20108%3A3-4&version=NIV; accessed September 25, 2024
https://www.biblegateway.com/passage/?search=Psalms%20106%3A1&version=NIV; accessed September 25, 2024
https://www.biblegateway.com/passage/?search=romans%2015%3A13&version=NIV; accessed September 25, 2024
https://www.biblegateway.com/passage/?search=Psalms%2021%3A16&version=NIV accessed September 25,

2024
https://www.biblegateway.com/passage/?search=Philippians%204%3A19&version=NIV; accessed September 25, 2024
https://www.biblegateway.com/passage/?search=jeremiah%2029%3A11&version=NIV; accessed September 25, 2024
https://www.biblegateway.com/passage/?search=1%20Corinthians%2015%3A57&version=NIV ; accessed September 25, 2024
https://www.biblegateway.com/passage/?search=Psalms%2037%3A%2023-24&version=NIV ; accessed September 25, 2024
https://www.biblegateway.com/passage/?search=Hebrews%2013%3A20-21&version=NIV; accessed September 25, 2024
https://www.biblegateway.com/passage/?search=Psalms%20119%3A105&version=NIV; accessed September 25, 2024
https://www.biblegateway.com/passage/?search=2%20Corinthians%202%3A14&version=NIV ; accessed September 25,. 2024
https://www.biblegateway.com/passage/?search=Colossians%203%3A16&version=NIV; accessed September 25, 2024

BIBLIOGRAPHY

https://www.biblegateway.com/passage/?search=hebrews%2012%3A2&version=NIV; accessed September 25, 2024

https://www.biblegateway.com/passage/?search=Matthew%205%3A16&version=NIV; accessed September 25, 2024

https://www.biblegateway.com/passage/?search=Proverbs%203%3A5-6&version=NIV; accessed September 25, 2024

https://www.biblegateway.com/passage/?search=Genesis%202%3A24&version=NIV; accessed September 25, 2024

https://www.biblegateway.com/passage/?search=Ephesians%205%3A25&version=NIV; accessed September 25, 2024

https://www.biblegateway.com/passage/?search=1%20john%204%3A12&version=NIV; accessed September 25, 2024

https://www.biblegateway.com/passage/?search=1%20Corinthians%2013%3A4&version=NIV; accessed September 25, 2024

https://www.biblegateway.com/passage/?search=Matthew%2019%3A6&version=NIV; accessed September 25, 2024

https://www.biblegateway.com/

passage/?search=1%20Corinthians%20 16%3A14&version=NIV; accessed September 25, 2024
https://www.biblegateway.com/ passage/?search=1%20peter%20 4%3A8&version=NIV; accessed September 25, 2024
https://www.biblegateway.com/ passage/?search=1%20peter%20 4%3A8&version=NIV; accessed September 25, 2024
https://www.biblegateway.com/ passage/?search=1%20john%20 4%3A7&version=NIV; accessed September 25, 2024
https://www.biblegateway.com/ passage/?search=romans%2012%3A9-9&version=NIV; accessed September 25, 2024
https://www.biblegateway.com/ passage/?search=Proverbs%20 19%3A21&version=NIV ; accessed October 17, 2024

3. *King James Version.* (n.d.). Gateway. Retrieved September 25, 2024, from http://gateway.comhttps://www.biblegateway.com/passage/?search=Genesis%201%3A27-28&version=KJV; accessed September 25, 2024
https://www.biblegateway.com/ passage/?search=Galatians%206%3A10-10&version=KJV; accessed September 25, 2024
https://www.biblegateway.com/ passage/?search=2%20timothy%204%3A7-

BIBLIOGRAPHY

8&version=KJV; accessed September 25, 2024 https://www.biblegateway.com/passage/?search=Deuteronomy%2028%3A%20 8&version=KJV; accessed September 25, 2024 https://www.biblegateway.com/passage/?search=hebrew%20 6%3A14&version=KJV; accessed September 25, 2024

4. New American Standard Bible (n.d). Gateway. Retrieved September 25, 2024, from https://www.biblegateway.com/passage/?search=Ephesians%205%3A15-17&version=NASB accessed September 25, 2024 https://www.biblegateway.com/passage/?search=Ephesians%205%3A28-31&version=NASB ; accessed September 25, 2024 https://www.biblegateway.com/passage/?search=Proverbs%2031%3A10-31&version=NASB ; accessed September 25, 2024 https://www.biblegateway.com/passage/?search=Ephesians%204%3A2-3&version=NASB, accessed September 25, 2024

5. North Carolina, U.S., Birth Indexes, 1800-2000 [database on-line] "database with images", Ancestry, https://www.ancestry.com/search/categories/bmd_birth/?name=james+henry_williams&event=_north+carolina-usa ;accessed August 23, 2024

6. https://www.ancestry.com/search/categories/34/?name=annie+v._hines&birth=1909-5-16_north+carolina-

usa_36&birth_x=10-0-0&father=richard_hines&name_x=s&searchMode=advanced; accessed October 17, 2024

7. Ancestry.com Operations Inc. (2007). *North Carolina, U.S., Death Indexes 1908-2004*. [[database on-line], "database with images", Ancestry. Retrieved September 23, 2024, from https://www.ancestry.com/search/categories/34/?name=annie+v_williams&birth=_north+carolina

8. Ancestry.com Operations Inc. *North Carolina, U.S., Death Certificates*, 1909-1976, [database on-line], "database with images", Ancestry, https://www.ancestry.com/discoveryui-content/view/795864%3A1121 , accessed August 24, 2024

9. North Carolina, *U.S. Marriage Records 1741-2011* [database on-line]. "database with images", Ancestry, *https://www.ancestry.com/search/collections/60548/?name=Annie+V _Williams&pg=3&birth=1909&death=1971& location=2&pcat=bmd_marriage&priority= usa&qh= ;accessed August 23, 2024*

10. North Carolina, *U.S., Marriage Records, 1741-2011*[database on-line], "database with images", Ancestry, https://www.ancestry.com/search/collections/60548/?name=james+henry_williams&pg=5&death=1971&f-C000000F=Bond&gender=f&location=2&name ; accessed August 24, 2024

11. North Carolina, U.S., Newspapers.com™ Stories

BIBLIOGRAPHY

and Events Index, 1800s, [database on-line], "database with images", Ancestry, https://www.ancestry.com/search/collections/62496/?name=james+henry_williams&event=1922-12_martin-north+carolina-usa_1925&pg= ; accessed August 26, 2024

12. OMG Hitched Team, ,(2024, May 03) , 59th Wedding Anniversary Ideas: Celebrating a Lifetime Together, https://omghitched.com/59th-wedding-anniversary-ideas/ , accessed September 28, 2024

13. Peterson, E. H. (1993,2002, 2018). *The Message Bible*. Gateway. Retrieved September 25, 2024, from http://gateway.com https://www.biblegateway.com/passage/?search=hebrews%2011%3A1-2&version=MSG; accessed September 25, 2024

14. The Lockman Foundation. (2015). *Amplified Bible*. Gateway. Retrieved September 25, 2024, from gateway.com https://www.biblegateway.com/passage/?search=1%20Timothy%203%3A8-11&version=AMP; accessed September 25, 2024 https://www.biblegateway.com/passage/?search=joshua%2024%3A15&version=AMP ; accessed September 25, 2024 https://www.biblegateway.com/passage/?search=james%201%3A17&version=AMP; accessed September 25, 2024

https://www.biblegateway.com/passage/?search=Proverbs%2018%3A22&version=AMP; accessed September 25, 2024

https://www.biblegateway.com/passage/?search=Lamentations%205%3A19&version=AMP; accessed September 25, 2024

15. The Lockman Foundation (1954, 1958, 1962, 1964, 1965, 1987). Amplified Bible Classic Edition. Gateway. Retrieved September 25, 2024, from gateway.com
https://www.biblegateway.com/passage/?search=Titus%202%3A4&version=AMPC,

16. Thomas Nelson. (1982). *New King James Version*. BibleGateway.com: A searchable online Bible in over 150 versions and 50 languages. Retrieved September 25, 2024, from https://www.biblegateway.com/passage/?search=Genesis%202%3A7-8&version=NKJV; accessed September 25, 2024

https://www.biblegateway.com/passage/?search=Genesis%202%3A18&version=NKJV; accessed September 25, 2024

https://www.biblegateway.com/passage/?search=Genesis%202%3A21-23&version=NKJV; accessed September 25, 2024

https://www.biblegateway.com/passage/?search=Ephesians%205%3A23-25&version=NKJV; accessed September 25, 2024

BIBLIOGRAPHY

https://www.biblegateway.com/passage/?search=Ephesians%205%3A32-33&version=NKJV; accessed September 25, 2024
https://www.biblegateway.com/passage/?search=Psalms%2018%3A1-2&version=NKJV; accessed September 25, 2024
https://www.biblegateway.com/passage/?search=1%20peter%202%3A24&version=NKJV ; accessed September 25, 2024
https://www.biblegateway.com/passage/?search=Ephesians%205%3A32-33&version=NKJV; accessed September 25, 2024
https://www.biblegateway.com/passage/?search=Matthew%205%3A13&version=NKJV; accessed September 25, 2024
https://www.biblegateway.com/passage/?search=Psalms%2018%3A1-2&version=NKJV; accessed September 25, 2024
https://www.biblegateway.com/passage/?search=Deuteronomy%2028%3A1-6&version=NKJV; accessed September 25, 2024
https://www.biblegateway.com/passage/?search=Numbers%206%3A%2025-26&version=NKJV; accessed September 25, 2024
https://www.biblegateway.com/passage/?search=romans%2010%3A8-10&version=NKJV; accessed September 25, 2024

17. Tree-Facts, Gallery, Life Story, [database on-line], "database with images", Ancestry,

https://www.ancestry.com/family-tree/person/tree/172696605/person/412261333518/facts?_phsrc=lrA461&_phstart=success, accessed August 24, 2024

https://www.ancestry.com/family-tree/person/tree/172696605/person/412261489508/facts, accessed August 25, 2024

https://www.ancestry.com/family-tree/person/tree/172696605/person/412261492247/facts, accessed August 26, 2024

18. U.S., Find a Grave® Index, 1600s-Current , [database on-line], "database with images, Lehi, UT, USA:, Ancestry.com Operations, Inc., 2012. *http://www.findagrave.com/memorial , accessed August 23, 2024*

19. 1930 United States Federal Census, Ancestry.com Operations Inc, 2002, Provo, UT, USA, [database on-line], "database with images", Ancestry, https://www.ancestry.com/discoveryui-content/view/5277541%3A8908

20. Wedding year 1965 - Mink wedding - Poster 59 years of marriage ,FLTMfrance, https://fltmfrance.com/en/products/annee-de-mariage-1965-noces-de-vison-1965-affiche-cadeau-59-ans-de-mariage, accessed September 28, 2024